Witches'
Spell-A-Day
Almanac

Holidays & Lore
Spells, Rituals & Meditations

You can order Llewellyn books and annuals from *New Worlds*,
Llewellyn's catalog. To request a free copy of the catalog, call toll-free
1-877-NEW WRLD or visit our website at www.llewellyn.com.

ISBN: 978-0-7387-3773-7

Llewellyn is a registered trademark of Llewellyn Worldwide Ltd.
2143 Wooddale Drive
Woodbury, MN 55125

Printed in the United States of America

Contents

A Note on Magic and Spells

The spells in the *Witches' Spell-A-Day Almanac* evoke everyday magic designed to improve our lives and homes. You needn't be an expert on magic to follow these simple rites and spells; as you will see if you use these spells throughout the year, magic, once mastered, is easy to perform. The only advanced technique required of you is the art of visualization.

Visualization is an act of controlled imagination. If you can call up in your mind a picture of your best friend's face or a flag flapping in the breeze, you can visualize. In magic, visualizations are used to direct and control magical energies. Basically the spellcaster creates a visual image of the spell's desired goal, whether it be perfect health, a safe house, or a protected pet.

Visualization is the basis of all good spells, and as such it is a tool that should be properly used. Visualization must be real in the mind of the spellcaster so it allows him or her to raise, concentrate, and send forth energy to accomplish the spell.

Perhaps when visualizing you'll find that you're doing everything right, but you don't feel anything. This is common, for we haven't been trained to acknowledge—let alone utilize—our magical abilities. Keep practicing, however, for your spells can "take" even if you're not the most experienced natural magician.

You will notice also that many spells in this collection have a somewhat "light" tone. They are seemingly fun and frivolous, filled with rhyme and colloquial speech. This is not to diminish the seriousness of the purpose, but rather to create a relaxed atmosphere for the practitioner. Lightness of spirit helps focus energy; rhyme and common language help the spellcaster remember the words and train the mind where it is needed. The intent of this magic is indeed very serious at times, and magic is never to be trifled with.

Even when your spells are effective, magic won't usually sparkle before your very eyes. The test of magic's success is time, not immediate eye-popping results. But you can feel magic's energy for yourself by rubbing your palms together briskly for ten seconds, then holding them a few inches apart. Sense the energy passing through them, the warm tingle in your palms. This is the power raised and used in magic. It comes from within and is perfectly natural.

Among the features of the *Witches' Spell-A-Day Almanac* are an easy-to-use "book of days" format; new spells specifically tailored for each day

of the year (and its particular magical, astrological, and historical energies); and additional tips and lore for various days throughout the year—including color correspondences based on planetary influences, obscure and forgotten holidays and festivals, and an incense of the day to help you waft magical energies from the ether into your space. Moon signs, phases, and voids are also included to help you find the perfect time for your rituals and spells.

Enjoy your days, and have a magical year!

Spell–A–Day Icons

 New Moon

 Meditation, Divination

 Full Moon

 Money, Prosperity

 Abundance

 Protection

 Altar

 Relationship

 Balance

 Success

 Clearing, Cleaning

 Travel, Communication

 Garden

 Air Element

 Grab Bag

 Earth Element

 Health, Healing

 Fire Element

 Home

 Spirit Element

 Heart, Love

 Water Element

Spells at a Glance by Date and Category*

	Health, Healing	Protection	Success	Heart, Love	Clearing, Cleaning	Home	Meditation, Divination
Jan.	11, 30	5, 13, 28	7, 25, 27	1	9, 14, 17	20, 21	8
Feb.	4, 17, 26	9, 12, 23	19, 25	7, 14		8, 24	10, 16, 27
March	5, 8	4, 10, 22	9, 11, 14, 24, 25	23, 28	6, 7, 12, 21, 29		30
April	4	6, 30	1, 17		14	19	18, 23, 26
May		12, 16	11	6, 9, 26, 27		19	
June	10	14, 22, 30			19		1, 2, 4, 23
July		5, 10, 14	4, 7, 8, 13, 22	16, 20	3, 21, 30	11	1, 18, 26, 28
Aug.	6, 16	10, 19, 29	7, 31	8, 15			1, 13, 20
Sept.	4, 11, 18	1, 25, 27	15	2, 14	23	6	7, 8, 10, 20
Oct.	11, 14, 22	16, 23, 30	10	19, 26	6, 20	4	3, 5, 25
Nov.	24, 28, 30	6, 12	9, 18, 20, 26	13	17, 21		8, 25
Dec.	17	10, 14	5, 8, 9		6, 25, 31	16, 20, 23	13, 15, 24, 28

*List is not comprehensive.

2018

Year of Spells

January

Happy New Year! The calendar year has begun and even though we may be in the depths of winter (in the Northern Hemisphere) or the height of summer (in the Southern Hemisphere), we stand at the threshold of fifty-two weeks filled with promise. Legend has it that this month is named to honor the Roman god Janus, a god of new beginnings and doorways, but it is also associated with Juno, the primary goddess of the Roman pantheon. Juno was said to be the protectress of the Roman Empire, and Janus (whose twin faces look to both the past and the future simultaneously) encourages new endeavors, transitions, and change in all forms. Since this month marks the beginning of the whole year, we can plant the seeds for long-term goals at this time, carefully plotting the course of our future success.

In the United States, there are three important holidays occurring in January: New Year's Day, Martin Luther King Jr. Day, and Inauguration Day. Each of these days exemplifies powerful change and transition. The dawn of a new year heralds a fresh start, and whether snow-covered or bathed in summer heat, January offers renewed possibilities for all.

Michael Furie

January 1

Monday

2nd ♊

☽ → ♋ 3:10 am

Full Moon 9:24 pm

Color of the day: Gray
Incense of the day: Rosemary

New Year's Day – Kwanzaa ends

On Target Spell

I don't know about you, but I tend to create lofty goals for myself every new year. Not only do I plan on losing that extra holiday weight, but I plan to train to run a marathon, create a magnificent work of art, and maybe finish that novel I've been working on. Alas, too many resolutions can set us up for a huge…fail.

Let's focus on one realistic New Year's resolution this year. This spell can help.

On a piece of paper, draw a full round circle, keeping your resolution fully in your mind. Continue drawing smaller circles within your large circle until you have created a target. In the middle, write your resolution. As you focus on this intent, repeat these words:

I can do this.

This goal is mine.

I can do this.

I am divine.

Keep your target intention somewhere visible until your goal is met.

Monica Crosson

NOTES:

January 2
Tuesday

3rd ♋

☽ v/c 5:46 pm

Color of the day: Black
Incense of the day: Ginger

New Year Prosperity Spell

At the new year, we often look back on habits we wish to change. This spell helps us to acknowledge things we do that can sabotage our prosperity, such as frivolous spending.

On your altar, place a large green candle, some nuts or dried beans, and a dollar bill. Place the nuts or beans on top of the dollar bill; these are to remind you that you have all the resources you need to meet your daily needs without spending money.

For the rest of the month, light the green candle each day and think of one way you can avoid spending money that day. Can you make dinner at home instead of getting takeout? Can you repair that hole in your jeans instead of getting a new pair? Can you read a book instead of shopping the online holiday sales? Remember, we usually don't really need many of the things we buy.

Each day you light the candle, count your blessings and be aware of how little you need to survive and be happy.

The beans or nuts represent the abundance and bounty in your life—family, friends, health, work—all of which are more important than money.

Peg Aloi

NOTES:

 January 3
Wednesday

3rd ♋

☽ → ♌ 2:23 am

Color of the day: White
Incense of the day: Lilac

Looking Back, Looking Ahead

January is named for Janus, the Roman god whose two faces look backward and forward. On your altar, set Janus or your two favorite gods or goddesses back to back. Have pen and paper handy. Light a black and a white candle. Cast your circle. Your intention is to examine the year just passed. Write down things you've done or said that you regret. Speak these words:

Great Janus, I'm looking at last year. These are things that I regret. I cannot undo or unsay them, but I can express regret and apologize.

Read each regret aloud, then burn each one in the flame of the black candle.

Now consider this new year. On paper, white down your pledges to do better and read them out loud. Clip them together and keep them where you can read them as often as necessary. Say:

Great Janus, I pledge to do better this year. When I'm standing on the edge of stupidity, please remind me of my pledge.
Barbara Ardinger

 January 4
Thursday

3rd ♌

☽ v/c 6:10 pm

Color of the day: Crimson
Incense of the day: Clove

Simple Morning Blessing

Even when we are too busy to perform a full-fledged ritual, we can still start off our morning with some magic. To imprint a desire into the unfolding pattern of the day, this technique can be effective.

Upon waking, form an idea of how you would like the day to proceed, and once the image and feeling are strong, reach your dominant hand up, tracing a pentagram in the air above you and visualizing a bright electric-blue energy. Start at the top point, moving down to the bottom-left point, then the upper right, left, lower right, and finally back to the top, completing the pentagram. Allow the power to linger in the air for a moment, then visualize the pentagram descend, bathing you in this energy so that the magic is absorbed into your being. To seal the spell, say:

Charged with power to light my way, magic bless me throughout this day.
Michael Furie

January 5
Friday

3rd ♌

☽ → ♍ 3:12 am

Color of the day: Purple
Incense of the day: Vanilla

Demon Banishing

According to legends of the people of Cypress, mischievous demons called *kalikandjari* arrive on Christmas Day and scheme and play pranks on people. Today is the day they depart, it is said.

In honor of this legend, it seems like a good day to do a good heavy clearing of the home in order to prevent any such little nasties from moving in, or perhaps to usher a few out! A good round of dragon's blood incense, followed by frankincense and myrrh, will do nicely. Walk through the home counterclockwise with the burning incense, and perhaps follow it up with some loud noise by ringing bells or banging pots and pans.

In many cultures, this is a traditional practice this time of year for banishing malevolent and stale energies. Some cultures also leave an offering outside and away from the home to lure mischievous spirits away from the dwelling.

Blake Octavian Blair

January 6
Saturday

3rd ♍

☽ v/c 9:51 pm

Color of the day: Blue
Incense of the day: Ivy

A Water Blessing

According to the Eastern Orthodox Church, today is considered the day when Christ was baptized. In some areas, crosses are placed in the sea, then divers dive down to find them and return them to dry land. Prayers are also said to bless sailors. In ancient Egypt, Pagans used this day to give thanks to the Nile.

Today is a good day to use water to bless your altar and ritual tools. Pour some bottled spring water into a clear glass bowl. Stir it three times with your hand. Dip any magical tools you wish to bless into the water, then sprinkle some on your altar too. As you do your blessing, say:

Water, water, clear and pure,

*Let the cleansing protection
you give these tools endure.*

Save the water and use it for other purification or blessing rituals.

James Kambos

 January 7
Sunday

3rd ♏

☽ → ♎ 7:15 am

Color of the day: Yellow
Incense of the day: Marigold

Get Organized

Remember the saying "New year, new you"? With or without set New Year's resolutions, take time to learn an organizing technique to support greater productivity and success in the year ahead. Why not set up a "bullet journal," a simple system that can help to magically transform your work habits, using an old-school analog system.

Find a notebook you like (either with or without lines). Sit quietly with it held close to your heart, and hear your heart's desires. Envision accomplishing those things you've dreamed about, supported by an easy yet effective planning tool. Go to www.tinyrayofsunshine.com/blog/bullet-journal-reference-guide for a free guide to setting up your own brilliant, affordable organizing system. In an hour you can read the quick guide, set up your own amazing tool for success, and jump in. Hold your new bullet journal to your heart and say:

Supported and blessed, I hold
the key to continued success.

Dallas Jennifer Cobb

 January 8
Monday

3rd ♎

4th Quarter 5:25 pm

Color of the day: Lavender
Incense of the day: Hyssop

Inducing Prophetic Dreams

The winter months are generally a time for introspective work. Utilize those energies and the lunar energies associated with Mondays and work on channeling prophetic dreams.

You will want to create a sachet that will aid you in your workings and place it under your pillow. A common herb that can be used is bay leaf. You can also add peppermint, mugwort, yarrow, holly, or cedar. Once you have combined the herbs into the bag, place it under your pillow. When you awaken from your slumber, you can write down any of the details of your dreams to interpret throughout the day.

Charlynn Walls

January 9
Tuesday

4th ♎

☽ v/c 11:13 am

☽ → ♏ 3:05 pm

Color of the day: White
Incense of the day: Bayberry

An Onion Spell to Peel Away Pain

Pain is multi-layered. Peel it away with this magical working. You'll need a pen, an onion—and maybe some tissues.

Write your fear, issue, or problem on the onion. Don't try to analyze it, just write the first words that come to mind. Visualize it, then peel away the words and the first layer of skin. Now search your heart and see what rises to the surface. Write that on the exposed skin, visualize it, and peel it off. Continue exposing layers and writing down the revelations that come with each pass, then peel them away. Speak each revelation as you write it. Peeling the onion may make you cry, but this isn't a bad thing; tears are cleansing.

When only the onion's core is left, bury it and all of the layers, letting the earth purify the energy at the heart of your dilemma.

Natalie Zaman

▽ **January 10**
Wednesday

4th ♏

Color of the day: Brown
Incense of the day: Honeysuckle

Healing Spell for Mother Earth

Gather some clean, dry garden soil and place it in a large bowl. Add some coffee grounds and chopped-up leaf matter, and mix well. Fill a small pitcher or spouted measuring cup with a cup or so of water. Draw a "river path" through the dirt with your finger. Inscribe a green candle and a blue one with symbols or runes of healing. After you light them, pour the water into the river and say:

Her blood is the water, and it's healing-blue. The earth is her body and it's healing-green. May the Mother be healed of all that's unclean.

Continue chanting, mixing the water into the soil until lightly damp. Let the power peak, sending the energy into the damp soil. Afterward, sprinkle the charged soil wherever you feel the earth needs healing.

Thuri Calafia

January 11

Thursday

4th ♏

☽ v/c 9:53 am

Color of the day: Green
Incense of the day: Jasmine

GG's Toddy

Beautiful as the winter season can be, it's also prime time for cold and flu viruses to attack. Fortunately, we magic people can fight back! One of my favorite healing weapons is my grandmother's healing toddy.

To make the toddy, squeeze the juice of one-half lemon into a warmed mug. Add a tablespoon of honey and a half teaspoon of grated raw ginger. My GG added a jigger (probably over-flowing) of whiskey or brandy; you can leave this out if you prefer. Fill the mug with near-boiling water and stir well, stirring sunwise (deosil). As you stir, repeat:

Lemons full of vitamin C,

Heat of ginger, honeybees,

Whiskey, soulful, rich, and warm,

Keep my body safe from harm.

Sip the toddy while it's as hot as pos-sible, breathing the steam as you do. Envision its healing qualities imbuing your body with protective vigor.

Susan Pesznecker

 January 12

Friday

4th ♏

☽ → ♐ 2:04 am

Color of the day: Pink
Incense of the day: Thyme

Bye-Bye Bills

Did you make a New Year's resolution to get out of debt this year? Move it along with some magical help to make your bills disap-pear. You will need a copy of your bills (don't use the originals) or a list of whom you owe and how much, a lighter, and a fire-safe container. After dark, take your supplies outside. Begin by tearing the copies or your list into thin strips. As you do so, chant:

I shred these bills down in size.

Add all of the strips to the fire-safe container. Light the pile of strips on fire. While it burns, chant:

I burn these bills down to nothing.

When the fire has gone out, toss the ash into the air and say:

Wind, take what is left behind.
Bye-bye, bills, so mote it be.

Kerri Connor

January 13
Saturday

4th ♐

Color of the day: Black
Incense of the day: Sandalwood

Knights Templar Protection

It was on this day in 1128 that the Knights Templar were officially sanctioned by Pope Honorius II. The Knights Templar were a fierce military organization and were declared "God's Army," or "Soldiers of Christ." This spell offers uncomplicated yet proven protection. Don't let its simplicity fool you! If you're going through a patch of bad luck or feel that someone's holding something against you, this will set things right.

You'll need a token that you usually wear. An amulet is great, but even a pendant, a ring, or your fitness tracker will work. Bend down on one knee, focus on your deity, and while holding your chosen item in your non-dominant hand, repeat this chant:

Lord, in all your glory,
protect me with your grace.

Repeat the chant until you feel your deity's peace descending upon you, and let your charmed item recall this protection whenever it needs a boost.

Charlie Rainbow Wolf

January 14
Sunday

4th ♐

☽ v/c 3:48 am
☽ → ♑ 2:42 pm

Color of the day: Gold
Incense of the day: Frankincense

Paper Purge

The waning Capricorn moon loves diligent purging activities. There is great power in a good paper purge, as it creates the space for a greater level of order and personal success.

So gather your junk mail, old journals and notebooks, and leftover lists. Light a white candle and a stick of sage or frankincense incense, and recycle, shred, and/or burn until all your unnecessary paper is banished from your home and life. As you do so, feel that you are breaking up old patterns, habits, and conditions and releasing the energy and power they formerly held in thrall. On a very deep level, sense that you are creating serenity within and around you and creating a vacuum into which fresh ideas, wealth streams, and beautiful life conditions will naturally flow. Finish by picking up the incense and (safely) wafting the smoke around your body and aura.

Tess Whitehurst

January 15
Monday

4☿ ♑

Color of the day: Silver
Incense of the day: Lily

Martin Luther King Jr. Day

World Peace Spell

Use this spell to honor the memory of Martin Luther King Jr. You'll need a light-blue pillar candle and a peace-attracting herb such as lavender. Place the candle on your altar, then sprinkle some of the lavender around the candle and on the floor around you. Light the candle. Gaze at the flame and visualize planet Earth as it appears in photos taken from outer space. Ground and center, then say:

> We are one, we all live
> beneath the same sun,
>
> May peace come to everyone.
>
> We are one, we all live beneath
> the same moon and stars,
>
> May peace come to every
> country, near and far.

After performing this spell, greet everyone with a smile. Offer assistance to anyone who may need help. Naturally, this spell won't work overnight, but think how powerful it would be if thousands of us performed it on this day!

James Kambos

 January 16
Tuesday

4☿ ♑

New Moon 9:17 pm

Color of the day: Maroon
Incense of the day: Geranium

A Chamomile New Moon Spell

Happy new moon! As you may know, the new moon is a time for vision and internal work. Additionally, when the moon is "new," it is also conjunct the sun. For this reason, the moon and sun are in the same zodiac sign at every new moon (unlike at the full moon, when the moon is in the sun's opposing sign). Today, Luna and Sol are both in the sign of Capricorn. This is an intelligent and resourceful sign whose energy grants us the ability to get to work!

To utilize this evening's energy, brew some nice chamomile tea. Find a large crystal or a favorite mystical gemstone and plop it into the mug (just be careful not to swallow the stone!). As the tea steeps, breathe in the vapors and envision the mug glowing with a dark violet hue. Chant the words *Capricorn*, *vision*, and *insight* into the steeping elixir. When you drink the tea, sit in your favorite chair and turn off all the lights. See which visions come to your attention!

Raven Digitalis

January 17
Wednesday

1st ♑

☽ v/c 1:30 am

☽ → ♒ 3:32 am

Color of the day: Yellow
Incense of the day: Lavender

What's Past Is (and Should Be) Done

L ook back at last year again. What should be buried and forgotten? Your intention is to bury the old stuff.

Set Athena and an earth goddess on your altar. Add a small, new plant and a flowerpot filled with potting soil. Light a red candle for root chakra energy. Cast your circle. Have paper and a pen handy as you comb through your memories and find things that need to be buried so Mother Earth can recycle them. Write them down, then speak these words:

What's done is done.

I am burying _____
from last year.

What's buried is safely gone.

Let it dissolve in the soil.

Let it be recycled.

Let it help this plant grow.

Let it change my life.

Burn what you wrote in the flame of the candle, then drop the ashes into the flowerpot. Mix them in with the soil. Plant the new plant and open your circle.

Barbara Ardinger

NOTES:

January 18

Thursday

1st ♒

Color of the day: Turquoise
Incense of the day: Nutmeg

The Quiet Midwinter

January is when "true" winter begins and the weather in the northern regions begins to turn much colder. After a busy holiday season, we want to slow down and hibernate. We can use the quiet, dormant energy of winter to do magical work, tapping into our inner depths to kindle the heat and light of creativity. This can help prevent depression and restlessness from setting in. Getting some exercise and spending time outside is a huge help to prevent seasonal depression, but spellwork can help focus our energy.

Do this working at noon, when the sun is at its zenith. Even if it's not sunny out, look up in the sky and try to sense the sun's position directly above you. Close your eyes and imagine the heat and light of the sun on your face. Let the sun's warmth and power flow over you; visualize yourself outdoors in summer doing this, imagining the sun's intensity. Wrap your arms around yourself to "hold in" the sun's energy, and draw upon this energy when you feel the gloomy dark of winter pressing down.

Peg Aloi

January 19

Friday

1st ♒

☽ v/c 6:52 am
☽ → ♓ 3:26 pm
☉ → ♒ 10:09 pm

Color of the day: Rose
Incense of the day: Rose

Tea of Plenty

This simple ritual to promote abundance and general prosperity utilizes regular tea, whole wheat toast, and a bit of butter. Tea (whether black, green, oolong, or white) contains the energy of prosperity. Wheat carries the energy of abundance, and butter is attuned to transformation. Sitting down with a freshly brewed cup of tea and some buttered toast can be an opportunity to partake of the magic of abundance.

As the water heats up, hold the tea bag (or tea strainer) and cultivate a sense of abundance. While the tea steeps, make the toast, and as you butter it, again focus on abundance. Before the first sip, say:

*Abundance and growth now
come forth. I take into myself
the power of plenty.*

Finish the tea and toast and try to hold the feeling of abundance as strongly as possible.

Michael Furie

January 20
Saturday

1st ♓

Color of the day: Indigo
Incense of the day: Pine

Gabija Bread Blessing

For most of us, winter's grip holds tight to the surrounding countryside. We keep to indoor pursuits, which, for our family, includes making bread. Nothing tastes better on a cold winter day than warm, homemade bread with butter and a bowl of soup. During these dark days of winter, comfort food most definitely helps keep spirits high.

Before slicing into your beautiful loaf, ask Gabija for a blessing. Gabija is a Lithuanian hearth goddess, protector of the fire and of the grain. With the advent of Christianity, Gabija was identified as Saint Agnes, who safeguarded homes from fire and was the patron saint of virgins.

Lay your hands over the bread and say:

Gabija of the hearth and of the grain, bless this bread

To keep us strong through the long winter days ahead.

Bless our hearts with your loving flame.

Help our minds keep bright until spring's reign.

Monica Crosson

 January 21
Sunday

1st ♓

☽ v/c 8:13 pm

Color of the day: Yellow
Incense of the day: Heliotrope

Brigid Invocation

The pre-Christian Irish goddess Brigid (pronounced "breed") is guardian of the home and known for her intellect, wisdom, and craft skills. She is also a protectress of sacred flame—literally and metaphorically. The long, cold nights of January find many of us seeking ways to keep warm. An appeal to Brigid can protect us through those chilly nights.

Sit in a dark room and light a single candle. Sit quietly, experiencing the darkness. Focus on the flame, scrying for any meanings that come. Repeat:

Dearest Brigid, keeper of hearth and home, protectress of all, font of love and wisdom,

Be with me through this long night.

Bless me as I sleep through winter's cold embrace.

Nurture my inner fire, sustaining life and filling me with warmth.

Give me the hope that spring will return, and with it

A promise of light and warmth.

To this I appeal. So mote it be.

Susan Pesznecker

January 22
Monday

1st ♓

☽ → ♈ 1:27 am

Color of the day: Ivory
Incense of the day: Neroli

Vino for Abundance

Today is Saint Vincent's Day, a saint associated with wine and all workers related to the vineyards throughout the Côte de Beaune and Côte de Nuits regions of France. The festival was an important one, and great effort was put by all into the celebration, as it was said that the year's grape harvest would mirror the success (or failure) of the festival. Grapes are associated magically with fertility and prosperity and thus abundance. Today, pour yourself a glass of your favorite wine (or non-alcoholic sparkling juice), light a candle, raise your glass in a toast, and chant:

*Saint Vincent, to you this
day we call upon*

*To allow our abundance
to continue on.*

*From the blessed grapes we
do harvest sacred wine.*

*A blessing of abundance
we do ask from the divine!*

Blessed be. So mote it be.

Now, enjoy your sacred libation!

Blake Octavian Blair

January 23
Tuesday

1st ♈

☽ v/c 11:16 pm

Color of the day: Red
Incense of the day: Cedar

Create a Charm Stone

To create a charm stone, first think of a wish. It could be a new home or financial stability, for example. Next, pray that you'll find a charm stone to help you with your need. Then be on the lookout for one. You may find it in your yard or while hiking. When you find it, you'll feel drawn to it. Charm stones don't need to be gemstones. Any rock will do as long as it "speaks" to you.

Once you have your stone, hold it and pray that your wish comes true. Always keep your charm stone in a box, or wrapped in fabric and in a drawer. Don't leave it on your altar or let anyone else use it. You can use a charm stone again, as long as it says it will help you. If a charm stone stops working, gently return it to the earth.

James Kambos

▽ January 24
Wednesday

1st ♈

☽ → ♉ 8:39 am

2nd Quarter 5:20 pm

Color of the day: Topaz
Incense of the day: Bay laurel

Golden Dreams

An earthy element, gold is grounding as well as a talisman for success and an amulet of deity. Today, on the 170th anniversary of the start of the California Gold Rush, draw on gold's energy to make your deepest dreams come true.

First, bathe yourself in the golden light of the sun—even if it's cloudy outside! (Remember, sometimes gold is hidden; many a prospector dug and panned to find gold.)

Next, visualize your desire and perceive it in shades of lustrous, luminous gold. If you have a piece of gold such as a coin or a piece of jewelry, hold it in your hand to help you transfer its energy to your vision. When you have the image clear in your mind, shout this spell aloud to seal it:

Eureka!

Repeat often until your desire comes to pass.

Natalie Zaman

① January 25
Thursday

2nd ♉

☽ v/c 10:17 pm

Color of the day: Purple
Incense of the day: Balsam

Royal Integrity

Historically, this is the date on which King Henry married Anne Boleyn—and we all know how that turned out! This spell will help you keep your head in trying situations. Be careful, though, because there's karma involved here, and you will need to accept responsibility for your actions—and their consequences.

For this spell, all you need is a mirror. A hand mirror works best, and it's also good if you have one specifically for magical purposes, rather than your bathroom mirror. Do this spell in broad daylight, not at night or twilight. Gaze into the mirror and repeat this chant:

By light of day my works be known,

And in this glass my true self shown

That I may walk in strength and faith,

The shadows not my spirit take.

Charlie Rainbow Wolf

January 26
Friday

2nd ♉

☽ → ♊ 12:40 pm

Color of the day: Coral
Incense of the day: Violet

honoring Your Partner

Today is National Spouses Day, so it's a great time to venerate your partner. Spouses are the individuals who hold our spirit and heart close to their own. Take a moment to honor your connection to one another and reaffirm that bond. Include your partner in this rite.

On your altar place two candles: one that represents you and one that represents your partner. You will also need one candle that represents the bond you share with one another. Next, each of you lights your own candle and says:

This light represents
my spirit and heart.

Now the two of you light the center candle from your two separate flames, saying:

Let our spirits mingle, bringing
understanding, passion, and love.

Charlynn Walls

January 27
Saturday

2nd ♊

Color of the day: Gray
Incense of the day: Sage

A Visualization for Success in Your Day

Do you ever wake up feeling exhausted or insecure? Sometimes our bodies go into healing mode during sleep, making it difficult to meet the demands of the day. If this occurs, try scheduling some extra sleepy time in the near future. In the meantime, give this visualization a try.

Take a few minutes to stretch the muscles, perform hatha (physical) yoga, and otherwise get the blood flowing. Take a shower, drink some tea or coffee, and start your day. To give yourself an additional boost of energy to succeed despite the lethargy, pull energy from the ground and sky. If you are on your way to work or an appointment, take a quick minute to put your bare feet on the earth and use your hands to draw up Mother Earth's healing essence. Next, reach upward and pull in the boundless energy of Father Sky. Visualize the two energies swirling in your chest and radiating throughout your body and mind. Breathe deeply. Conclude by giving thanks and saying:

As above, so below.
As within, so without.

Raven Digitalis

January 28
Sunday

2nd ♊

☽ v/c 5:39 am

☽ → ♋ 1:57 pm

Color of the day: Amber
Incense of the day: Eucalyptus

Data Protection Day

Today is Data Protection Day, also known as Data Privacy Day. This day was founded to raise awareness about keeping our personal and business information safe online. Modern magical practitioners can employ the energetic momentum of this mainstream observance to protect against identity theft and other forms of digital crime. To do so, first take a little time to investigate how you can get even wiser about keeping your online banking and other sensitive online information safe and sound. Then call on the angel of mathematics, words, and energetic encoding: Archangel Metatron. Request and envision that he lock your data up tight from anyone who would seek to abuse it. Then call on Archangel Michael to hermetically seal it in a fiery wall of protection. Finish by changing the desktop photo on all your devices to the protective rune Algiz. Leave it there for at least one full moon cycle.

Tess Whitehurst

January 29
Monday

2nd ♋

Color of the day: White
Incense of the day: Narcissus

Tree Pose

Start your week off with some balance work. Stand in yoga tree pose. While holding the pose, experiment with your arm placement. Begin with hands at prayer, then move them about, outstretched to the sides, up over your head, like the branches of a tree. As you do so, notice how you begin to lose your balance, but your body fights to regain it. If your foot drops, go ahead and start again. Fight to keep the balance in your pose.

Think about what areas of your life feel out of balance. How can you manipulate your life to bring your balance back? When the branches of your life start swaying in the breeze, how do you continue to hold yourself upright? Spend some time visualizing your life in perfect balance. What does that look like for you?

Kerri Connor

January 30
Tuesday

2nd ♋

☽ v/c 11:40 am

☽ → ♌ 1:53 pm

Color of the day: Scarlet
Incense of the day: Cinnamon

Self-healing Spell

With the waxing moon going into Leo today, it's a good time to consider our relationship with our physical body and how that relates to our health. If we have ailments or illnesses, if we want to head off the colds and flu bug going around our workplace or school, or if we just want to improve our health in general, heartfelt spellwork can help.

Make an herbal charm (you can even think of it as a medicine bag) by adding healing and vitalizing herbs such as cinnamon, allspice, and ginger, or calming herbs such as lavender, valerian, and hops. Tie the herbs up in a cotton bag of an appropriate color (such as red for healing blood and tissues, pink for lungs, blue to calm emotions, etc.). As you make the charm, visualize yourself in perfect health, your ailment vanished. Wear the charm until you feel better, then release the herbs on the wind.

Thuri Calafia

 January 31
Wednesday

2nd ♌

Full Moon 8:27 am

Color of the day: Brown
Incense of the day: Marjoram

Lunar Eclipse

A Quickening Spell

The second full moon of the year has many names: Snow Moon, Moon of Ice, Bear Moon, Quickening Moon, Little Famine Moon, and Bony Moon. This one occurs in Leo, a sign known for shining a personal spotlight. Prepare to view tonight's total lunar eclipse either outdoors or indoors. A lunar eclipse is symbolic of our shadow self, so ruminate about what "shadow" you want to shine the Leo spotlight on. Cast this spell as the earth passes between the sun and moon. As a shadow creeps across the moon, name it. For example:

I am afraid of abandonment.

At the peak of the eclipse, be still. Breathe deeply and simply be with your shadow. Feel it. As light creeps across the moon, identify the shadow's strength:

I am autonomous and self-sufficient.

In the spotlight of the full Quickening Moon, know that your strength is illuminated.

Dallas Jennifer Cobb

February

The word *February* is based on the Latin *februa* and refers to the Roman festival of purification of the same name. This festival later became integrated with February's infamous Lupercalia. Since ancient times, February has been observed as a month of cleansing, cleaning, purification, and preparation for the warm months ahead. We see the Celtic Imbolg (Candlemas) celebrated in February to perpetuate the summoning of solar light. In many parts of the world at this time, the promise of sunlight seems bleak, even imaginary. The world around us is slowly awakening from its wintery slumber, and some semblance of excitement begins to grow in the hearts of those attuned to the seasonal tides.

Daylight hours are short in February, so this time of year can sometimes feel depressive. We must actively cultivate our inner light through regular exercise, solid sleep, meditation, yoga, ritual, studying, artwork, and planning ahead for the year. When performing magickal work this month, remember that your energy levels may be lower than usual and you must summon your own inner light to strengthen and illuminate your efforts. Do whatever it takes to stay on top of your game, keep energized, cultivate happiness, and embrace February's cleansing rebirth!

Raven Digitalis

February 1
Thursday

3rd ♌

☽ v/c 5:59 am

☽ → ♍ 2:13 pm

Color of the day: Green
Incense of the day: Apricot

A Cup of Cocoa for Saint Brigid

Today is Saint Brigid's Day, that goddess guised as a saint who is, among other things, the patroness of dairy maids (which connects her to the ewes coming into milk at this time of year). February also brings us Lupercalia, Juno Februata, and Valentine's Day, celebrations of the passion that sparks all month (perhaps with a bit of commercial help!).

Bring Brigid and love together with a hot chocolate spell. Add your favorite chocolate medium to a mug of warm milk (which will also ward off winter chills!). Stir the brew clockwise to invoke her, and speak this incantation:

Brigid, divine saint and goddess,

Bless me with your gracious goodness.

In milk is possibility,

In chocolate, love and empathy.

Come together on this day

To bring your light and love my way.

Toast the goddess and savor every sip, knowing you are blessed with love and potential.

Natalie Zaman

NOTES:

February 2

Friday

3rd ♍

Color of the day: White
Incense of the day: Orchid

Imbolc – Groundhog Day

Create a Magical Incense

Imbolc is a traditional fire festival. Prepare for it with this incense.

You'll need a combination of these Imbolc/winter-corresponding dry materials (bark and aerial parts should be in dried form): cedar bark, shavings, or essential oil; rowan leaves, berries, or bark; basil leaves; blackberry leaves or brambles; oak shavings, leaves, or bark; rosemary leaves or essential oil; whole or powdered cloves; cinnamon sticks or powder; mugwort; holly leaves or berries.

In addition, you'll need one or more of the following binders: grated beeswax, carrier oil (olive or sunflower are ideal), or your choice of resin.

Combine the dry materials in a mortar and pestle (or spice grinder) to create a uniform mixture. Add the binder to bring the incense together, whether in loose or "solid" form.

As you work, charge the incense by repeating:

Scents of ages, born of fire,
spells arise as will inspires.

Use your incense to usher in Imbolc.

Susan Pesznecker

 February 3

Saturday

3rd ♍

☽ v/c 2:07 am

☽ → ♎ 4:47 pm

Color of the day: Brown
Incense of the day: Patchouli

Finding Balance

With life so hectic and busy for so many of us, it can be hard to balance work, school, family, friends, romantic partner(s), and alone time. Take a moment to focus on what you need to recharge and realign your energies. Now take a pale-blue pillar candle and carve it with a large set of scales (the symbol for Libra), as the moon goes into Libra today and it's a good time for balancing energies. Next, carve symbols or words of all those various balls you're trying to keep in the air.

Anoint the candle with some lavender oil, for peace and harmony, and visualize all these different aspects of your life running smoothly. Focus clearly and strongly. Let the candle burn for several nights in a row, until it is gone (taking any necessary safety precautions). Be blessed.

Thuri Calafia

February 4

Sunday

3rd ♎

Color of the day: Gold
Incense of the day: Almond

Flu Defender

February is one of the high points for flu season, so make sure to take your vitamins, wash your hands, and be aware of your own germs spreading. (Being aware of your own spreading germs makes you more aware of everyone else's germs as well, making you more vigilant.)

At night, add the following mixture to a diffuser near your bed:

1 drop black pepper oil

1 drop clove oil

4 drops frankincense oil

5 drops peppermint oil

6 drops eucalyptus oil

Say this spell before going to bed:

Lady of strength,

Lady so bold,

Protect my home

From the illnesses of the cold.

Keep us warm and safe,

Healthy and well.

Kerri Connor

February 5

Monday

3rd ♎

☽ v/c 1:46 pm

☽ → ♏ 10:56 pm

Color of the day: Silver
Incense of the day: Clary sage

Clean Slate Spell

Snow is a common occurrence during the winter months and in the mountains. If you live in an area where snow is common, you can utilize that in your spells. If you live in a climate that does not typically have snow, you can create your own by shaving ice in a blender and then pouring that onto a flat surface.

For this spell, write out a word or phrase in the snow. Fresh snowfall will accumulate on the word or phrase and obliterate it, or you can wipe your hand through the snow to create the effect of a clean slate. This will give you a fresh start regarding the matter.

For example, you may want to quit a bad habit. So write the habit out in the snow with the intention that you are starting over and this will no longer be a part of your life. You are giving it up and the higher power will work with you to obscure this from your higher self.

Charlynn Walls

February 6

Tuesday

3rd ♏

Color of the day: Gray
Incense of the day: Bayberry

Music with a Message

Today is musical artist Bob Marley's birthday. Marley's music was known for conveying a variety of messages, so take the opportunity today to make a statement through song.

In honor of this well-loved artist, listen to a few of his songs today. Do any of them seem to speak to you about something in your life or a philosophy you have? Do some journaling on the topic, if you feel moved. Then do a bit of magick to work on that area of life. Cater your magick to your topic, but keep it simple, perhaps with a color-coordinated candle and oil. You can play your chosen Marley song as your spell candle burns down, reinforcing your intent.

Music is magick. Today, let Marley's magic be a catalyst for your own!

Blake Octavian Blair

 February 7

Wednesday

3rd ♏
4th Quarter 10:54 am

Color of the day: Topaz
Incense of the day: Honeysuckle

True Love Waits

Valentine's Day brings the opportunity for romance, and this spell increases your chances for love. It will not bring a reluctant lover to you, though, so don't try to control anyone's free will. This only works if the two of you have some chemistry and a real chance at creating a relationship.

You'll need two stones and a sunny windowsill for this spell. Put one stone in the left inside corner of the windowsill and the second stone in the far right corner. Every day, move the stones a little bit closer together, only a centimeter or so each time. As you move them, say the following chant:

Bit by bit, if it's meant to be,

You'll open your heart and come to me.

If this person truly is meant for you, then by the time the stones are together on the window, you'll be in each other's arms!

Charlie Rainbow Wolf

February 8
Thursday

4th ♏

☽ v/c 2:16 am

☽ → ♐ 8:53 am

Color of the day: White
Incense of the day: Carnation

Four Corners
Household Protection

The house and home are sacred. At home we can fully be ourselves and let loose. At home we can rejuvenate our bodies and minds. At home we can plan ahead for the future while we take a breath and find our center.

To add a little boost of protection and calming energy to your home, gather five stones of the same type. My suggestions include fluorite, agate (especially moss agate), amazonite, jasper, or turquoise. If nothing else, simply use five small quartz crystals.

Secure four of the stones in the corners of the house, whether buried outside or somehow affixed inside. Place the fifth stone as close to the center of the house as you can manage, equidistant from the others. Visualize the stones linking in a boxed X formation, creating a shield around the house and within. Visualize this connection any time to reinforce the magick.

Feel free to modify this spell for a bedroom or apartment in any manner your intuition guides you. Get creative and have fun!

Raven Digitalis

NOTES:

February 9
Friday

4th ♐

Color of the day: Rose
Incense of the day: Yarrow

A Snow and Stone Spell

You may use this ritual to end a habit or problem in your life. You'll need a small stone no larger than a walnut, some black paint, and some snow or crushed ice.

After you select your stone, paint it black as you focus on blocking or getting rid of your problem, then let it dry. Next, using snow or ice, form a ball around the stone. Place the snow/ice-covered stone outside where it won't be disturbed and say:

Snow [Ice] and stone, end my problem, and may it leave me alone.

Let the snow or ice melt naturally, even if it takes weeks. After the snow has melted, return and press the stone into the earth. Leave it undisturbed. Your problem will fade as the negative energy from the stone is harmlessly absorbed by Mother Earth.

James Kambos

February 10
Saturday

4th ♐

☽ v/c 11:38 am
☽ → ♑ 9:21 pm

Color of the day: Blue
Incense of the day: Magnolia

Simple Magic

Magic is like food. There are many different cultures, tastes, and techniques. Tools and ingredients can be obscure and difficult to find, or they can be everyday kitchen items. Preparation can be elaborate or simple. My household is busy, and mealtime is often time to "perform miracles"—to make a five-minute meal that tastes great and nourishes us. Magically, I rely on simple magic I can perform in a crisis—no lengthy preparations or hard-to-find ingredients.

Today, make your own simple magic spell. Take something you do every day (like showering or drinking tea) and turn it into a magic spell (for protection or invoking clarity and focus). Everyday objects and practices can anchor our consciousness, facilitate self-awareness, and remind us of our ability to choose change. Like a hot meal when you're hungry and tired, simple magic can transform energy. At the end of a long day, if it ain't simple, it won't work.

Dallas Jennifer Cobb

February 11
Sunday

4th ♍ VS

Color of the day: Orange
Incense of the day: Juniper

Eagle Spirit Bag for Courage

February is a great time to pack up the family and go birding. In my neck of the country, eagles can be seen dotting the nearby rivers and tributaries, feasting on spawning salmon. The eagle is a powerful symbol for courage, so why not bag up some of that eagle spirit power for a little spiritual pluck? You will need:

- A drawstring bag
- 1 to 2 eagle's claw seed pods (*Uncaria rhynchophylla*)
- A pinch of dried chili pepper
- A bloodstone

Put all of your ingredients in the drawstring bag. Hold the bag in your hands and focus on the eagle's inherent energies. Imagine yourself set free from insecurities and doubt. You are powerful and courageous. You can endure anything. Now say:

Eagle spirit, as my guiding power,

Set me free from anxiety's bower.

Lend me courage three times three,

As the spirit wills it, so mote it be!

Carry your eagle spirit bag with you as needed for extra courage.

Monica Crosson

NOTES:

✪ February 12
Monday

4th ♑

Color of the day: Gray
Incense of the day: Hyssop

Make a Smudge Stick for Protection

Choose fresh or dried materials to use for your smudge. Sprigs of cedar, fir, pine, sweetgrass, sage, juniper, and rosemary are especially good for protection work.

On a strip of paper, draw protective runes. Or write these words:

As the smoke surrounds me here,
keep me safe from harm and fear.

Gather the plant materials into a bundle, nestling the paper strip into the middle. Tie the bundle at the base with a thin cotton string. Wind the string around the bundle until you reach the tip, then wind back down to the base. Tie the string off and clip it close. Let the fresh bundle dry on your altar for seven to ten days before using.

To use, hold the bundle over a fire-proof dish or abalone shell and light it. Quickly blow out the flame and use the smoke to smudge and protect you, others, or a location, repeating the previous mantra.

Susan Pesznecker

🍂 February 13
Tuesday

4th ♑

☽ v/c 12:43 am
☽ → ♒ 10:11 am

Color of the day: Maroon
Incense of the day: Basil

Mardi Gras (Fat Tuesday)

Blessed Are We

Today is Mardi Gras, the last Christian feast before the Lenten fast. We Pagans aren't interested in a tortured god, but we can respect Jesus as a teacher. Go online and find (and print) the Beatitudes (Matthew 5:3–10) or open your Bible to the Sermon on the Mount.

Gather your covenmates. Set Sophia or Ma'at or another goddess of holy wisdom on your altar and cast your circle. Your intention is to understand how your life is filled with blessings. Invoke holy wisdom. Read the Beatitudes aloud. Now ask each member of your circle to speak aloud two or three examples of blessings in their lives using these words:

Blessed am I because _____.

Go around the circle two or three times giving examples of how your lives are blessed. Open your circle, and as you feast, talk about Beatitudes and blessings. Do any of your blessings echo the Beatitudes?

Barbara Ardinger

February 14

Wednesday

4th ≈

Color of the day: White
Incense of the day: Bay laurel

Valentine's Day – Ash Wednesday

Love in the Cards

This working encourages the full scope of love in our lives (romantic, familial, and friendship), bringing harmony. For this spell, you'll need these tarot cards: the Three of Swords, Three of Cups, Two of Cups, Ten of Cups, and the Lovers. Lay them on a table in a row in the order given, with the Three of Swords beginning on the left and the Lovers ending on the right.

Set a gray candle behind the left card, a pink candle next, a red one for the middle, light blue next, and a lavender candle at the right. The intent is to neutralize the left card while encouraging the power of the remaining cards. Light candles left to right, saying:

Releasing sorrow, cast away, nurturing friendship and true love; family harmony, here to stay; transcendent joy, blessed from above; for good of all and by free will, let this magic be fulfilled.

Michael Furie

 February 15

Thursday

4th ≈

☽ v/c 4:05 pm

New Moon 4:05 pm

☽ → ♓ 9:42 pm

Color of the day: Crimson
Incense of the day: Mulberry

Solar Eclipse

New Moon Spell for healthy habits

Winter is often a time when we try to correct unhealthy habits, particularly those surrounding diet and exercise. But the cold months are a hard time to diet, because we need to eat more to stay warm. We just want to binge on TV and junk food, right? But we can intentionally improve our eating habits without depriving ourselves. One way to do this is to eat with intention.

On this new moon, make some soup (plenty of easy recipes online!). A simple vegetable soup is perfect. When you're ready to eat dinner, set the table and sit down. Light a candle to suggest a ritual atmosphere. Eat the soup spoonful by spoonful, taking your time to really enjoy every aspect of it: how it looks, how it smells, the texture in your mouth, the taste. This new moon can mark the beginning of this new habit. Cultivating this mindfulness while eating can help us to avoid overeating or eating in a distracted way (such as in front of the TV or computer), which can lead to weight gain.

Peg Aloi

NOTES:

 February 16

Friday

1st ♓

Color of the day: Pink
Incense of the day: Mint

Lunar New Year (Dog)

An Animal Shelter Blessing

In the Chinese zodiac, Dog folk possess some of the best traits in human nature: loyalty, honesty, straightforwardness, and dependability. Usher in the Year of the Dog with a shelter and rescue blessing.

Make a crystal elixir by adding a rose quartz (for love), jade (for healing, health, and luck), and tiger's eye (for success and drive) to a cup of water. Let the stones imbue the water with their power over the night of Lunar New Year. Bless the shelter or rescue organization in person, or simply visualize it. Sprinkle the water in the sacred formation of your choice (like a spiral or star) with these words:

Bless this place with Dog energy, with love and loyalty, fierceness and friendship.

Bring to its doorstep plenty, prosperity, and loyal people called to do this necessary work.

May those who come here seeking companionship do so with honest intentions and a responsible heart.

So mote it be.

Natalie Zaman

February 17
Saturday

1st ♓

☽ v/c 5:14 pm

Color of the day: Indigo
Incense of the day: Rue

108 Stones for health and healing

For a variety of reasons, the number 108 is sacred in many paths of Eastern mysticism, including Hinduism, Buddhism, Sikhism, Jainism, and both tantric and yogic schools of thought. For this ritual, gather 108 small stones or pebbles, two containers to hold them, and a stick of your favorite incense.

Sit comfortably at a small table, with a bowl of stones in front of you to the left and an empty bowl to your right. Light the incense, take some deep breaths, and calm your mind. Get comfortable. Using your right hand, grab one stone or pebble. Visualize yourself and say:

> I send you love, healing,
> and happiness.

Then put the stone in the empty bowl. Do the same with the second stone, but this time visualize someone you know (even if you barely know them). Say the words while you project the energy toward the person.

Continue this with a different person (or animal) in mind each time, even if they are from your past

and even if they have crossed over. Conclude by casting the stones into a body of running water. This ritual generates beneficial karma for yourself while lending a bit of light to others in your life.

Raven Digitalis

NOTES:

February 18
Sunday

1st ♓

☽ → ♈ 7:05 am

☉ → ♓ 12:18 pm

Color of the day: Yellow
Incense of the day: Heliotrope

Sharpen Your Mind Spell

Today's Diana's Bow moon in Aries gives us all sorts of energy for pushing forward with new projects. Give a push toward mental clarity with this spell!

Choose a nice, clear crystal from your collection, or visit a local rock shop for a new crystal point. The best way to choose a crystal is to let it choose you. Sit in front of your altar and light a white or yellow candle. Holding the crystal in your left hand, project energy into it with your right hand. Say:

Guardian spirits of wisdom and air, bright winged creatures and mornings fair, send your powers to this crystal through me, by the grace of the gods—so mote it be!

Continue the chant until your crystal is buzzing with the energy. Keep the crystal on your person whenever you feel the need for a mental boost.

Thuri Calafia

February 19
Monday

1st ♈

Color of the day: Ivory
Incense of the day: Rosemary

Presidents' Day

Make Up Your Mind to Be Happy

Abraham Lincoln said, "Most folks are about as happy as they make up their mind to be." And according to the hermetic law of polarity, happy and unhappy—like other pairs of opposites—are simply two poles of the exact same thing. Although it sounds simplistic, we can envision our happiness level as a dimmer switch, and we can make the conscious decision to turn it up.

Close your eyes and see your inner happiness switch. If it's not all the way up, turn it up and see your world get brighter. Open your eyes and take some steps on the physical plane to turn up your happiness as well: get rid of old clutter, diffuse mood-boosting essential oil, bring in fresh flowers, or donate any decoration in your space that doesn't lift your spirits. And today, every time you have an opportunity to smile or laugh, take it!

Tess Whitehurst

February 20

Tuesday

1st ♈

☽ v/c 6:11 am

☽ → ♉ 2:12 pm

Color of the day: Red

Incense of the day: Ylang-ylang

Strength and Courage Spell

Some days you need a boost of strength and courage. That's okay. We all do from time to time, whether we show it outwardly or not.

For this spell, gather the following three items: a polished piece of bloodstone, an image of the Strength card from the tarot, and a white candle. Bloodstone vibrates with the energy of courage, which pairs nicely with the type of strength symbolized by the Strength card. We need not always exert brute force to be strong. We can use our will, compassion, and intellect to exert our strength.

Place the image of the Strength card upon your altar, with the candle and bloodstone atop it. Light the candle and visualize the bloodstone absorbing both the courageous light of the candle and the strength of the card. Carry the bloodstone with you.

Blake Octavian Blair

 February 21

Wednesday

1st ♉

Color of the day: Brown

Incense of the day: Lilac

Honoring the Shades

Ancient Romans observed this day as Feralia, which was the last of three festivals that honored the dead. They took offerings to the tombs and laid them out to appease the spirits. While we are not always able to take offerings to the tombs of our loved ones, we can still honor their spirits, commune with them, and provide offerings to them.

Begin by creating sacred space around the altar you will be working with. Call the names of the deceased you wish to honor. Take salt, bread, and flowers and place them in an offering bowl on your altar. The salt will keep them from lingering too long, the bread will nourish their soul, and the flowers will show your appreciation for their presence in your life. Invite them to stay for the day within that sacred space, and be open to any messages they may have.

Charlynn Walls

February 22
Thursday

1st ♉

☽ v/c 6:46 am

☽ → ♊ 7:07 pm

Color of the day: Turquoise
Incense of the day: Jasmine

The Earth Awakens

Traditionally on this day, maple trees are tapped and maple syrup production begins. Sap has begun to rise, and now the earth awakens! This ritual will allow you to help the earth awaken from its winter rest, and will help awaken your winter-weary spirit too.

First gather some soil in a flower-pot. If the ground is too frozen, then use potting soil. Place the potted soil before a fire or a lit orange candle. Sprinkle the soil lightly with water. Hold your hands over the soil, gaze at the fire or burning candle, and say:

Spring will come and summer too,

*Earth spirit, hear the
words I speak to you.*

Cold and silent you have laid,

Arise now from your winter grave.

*Let the life spirit in every plant
and seed begin to swell,*

Sustain us all, and keep us well.

End the ritual by scattering the soil outside.

James Kambos

February 23

Friday

1st ♊

2nd Quarter 3:09 am

Color of the day: Purple
Incense of the day: Rose

Beneficial Boundaries

Historically the Roman festival of Terminalia was held on February 23, honoring Terminus, the god who protected boundary markers. Today is a great day to invoke healthy boundaries, both physical and emotional, and consciously set them.

If you have neighbors, make an effort to exchange good energy with them. Even if you don't see them, you can do a quick shovel of their walkway or some other task. The act of doing good for your neighbor energetically sets the stage for a good relationship.

While you are doing simple physical tasks, take time to walk the boundary between your properties and invoke Terminus:

Terminus, guide us to live in peace.

I respect my neighbor;
may they respect me.

Protect our boundaries so
we can live in ease,

Terminus, now be here with me.

As you walk the property boundary, know that you are simultaneously setting your own healthy boundary and observing your neighbor's boundary.

Dallas Jennifer Cobb

NOTES:

February 24
Saturday

2nd ♊

☽ v/c 2:58 pm

☽ → ♋ 10:06 pm

Color of the day: Black
Incense of the day: Sandalwood

Cabin Fever Release

Home is where the heart is, but by the end of February, those who live in cold-winter states may be feeling anything but "homey." Cabin fever has set in and taken its toll, and people want to get out and have fun again. The holidays are over and boredom may be prevalent. Use this day to have some fun.

March is just around the corner, followed by spring, but it may still seem like a long way off. Have a fun game night to bring some cheer back into your life. Invite family and friends, Pagan or not. At the beginning of the evening, ask everyone to give thanks in their own way for something they appreciate. It may be about spending time with friends or family or something completely different. Sometimes we just need to let off steam and share reminders about the good in our lives.

Kerri Connor

February 25
Sunday

2nd ♋

Color of the day: Amber
Incense of the day: Marigold

The Parking Space Word

No matter where you live, if you drive a car, you need to park it somewhere—at home, at work, wherever you go. Whether you're at the mall or driving around a neighborhood that has more multi-family dwellings than there are parking spaces, you need to park your car.

As you search for that almost invisible parking space, speak the parking space word:

ZZZZZAAAAAAZZZZZ!

Speak it loud and with great energy. It seems to work best if you plan ahead and say where you want to park. Therefore, speak the parking space word when you turn a corner or enter the parking lot:

ZZZZZAAAAAZZZZZ!
Parking space at _____.

Be aware that the word works, but not always immediately. Sometimes you have to drive around the block or around the lot. Repeat the word every time you turn a corner. It will work.

Barbara Ardinger

February 26
Monday

2nd ♋

☽ v/c 4:51 pm

☽ → ♌ 11:42 pm

Color of the day: Lavender
Incense of the day: Neroli

Simple Vitality Potion

To shore up your energetic reserves and bring an added boost to your health, here is a quick recipe to try. Combine two tablespoons lemon juice, two tablespoons lime juice, and two tablespoons honey. Stir to combine, then add a cup of club soda or seltzer. Hold your hands over the mixture and charge it with white light, saying:

Pure white light from magical source, fill this potion with energy; strength and health are reinforced, with each sip, increased vitality.

Drink the potion and visualize its energy expanding throughout your body.

Michael Furie

 # February 27
Tuesday

2nd ♌

Color of the day: White
Incense of the day: Ginger

No-Brainer Day Meditation

No-Brainer Day was created by eventologist Adrienne Sioux Koopersmith as a day to give our brains a rest. If you must work, take plenty of coffee breaks and do not work overtime. When you get home, prepare a simple dinner and participate in activities that are enjoyable. As evening sets in, find a quiet spot in the house or garden and take time to focus on the things that bring you joy.

Gather some fresh freesia blooms (the official flower of No-Brainer Day) or incense to lift your spirits, and play your favorite soft music. Sit quietly and close your eyes. For this moment you are not your past or your future. You are only the present. There are no burdens for you here, but only joy. Focus on that joy for as long as you please.

Remember, you deserve this time. That's a no-brainer.

Monica Crosson

℣ebruary 28

Wednesday

2nd ♌

☽ v/c 6:13 pm

Color of the day: Yellow
Incense of the day: Lavender

Spell for Safe Travel

Winter can be a good time for leisure travel because there are often bargains offered during this slower travel season. Despite many modern technology innovations, travel seems more stressful now than ever before. With so much to keep track of, this added stress can take away from the enjoyment of travel or cause us to forget important items.

Before traveling, you can make and wear this charm, and use it to calm your energy when things get overwhelming. Take a three-inch square of blue fabric (silk, linen, or cotton work best). Inside the square, place the following items:

- A small hematite or amethyst stone

- A silver dime or other silver coin (an antique coin made entirely of silver is best)

- An acorn, a small pinecone, a pebble, or some other natural object taken from the vicinity of your home

- A small slip of paper with the word "HOME" written on it

Fold the fabric inward and tie the ends together firmly in a bundle with a long piece of ribbon that is long enough to tie into a necklace. Wear this charm while traveling and it will help you remain calm and focused.

Peg Aloi

NOTES:

Page 45

March

March is upon us! March is a month of unpredictable weather. Will the weather spirits decide to bring us a last hurrah of winter in the form of a blustery snowstorm or instead bring us signs of spring's beginning in the form of budding trees and perhaps rain showers sprinkled with mild, sunny days? There really is no telling! However, for those of us who follow the Wheel of the Year, the spring equinox is a time of new beginnings, regardless of the weather.

Rituals of spring and new beginnings will take place around the globe this month. Druids still gather at Stonehenge to welcome the rising sun on the morning of the equinox. March also is the time to celebrate the festival of Holi, popular in India and Nepal. People engage in paint fights, covering each other in festive splatters of vibrant color, welcoming the arrival of spring and all its vibrancy.

In March, however you choose to celebrate, work the magick of new beginnings!

Blake Octavian Blair

March 1
Thursday

2nd ♌

☽ → ♍ 12:57 am

Full Moon 7:51 pm

Color of the day: Green
Incense of the day: Clove

Purim

Creating Moon Water

Religious traditions around the world make use of holy water. A great mystique surrounds holy water and its creation; however, it's really quite simple to make. Holy water is any water that has been blessed or charged or that came from a sacred site. You have all the power necessary to create your own holy water, and today—a full moon—is a great day to do it!

Take a glass bottle with a tight-fitting lid, fill it with clean water, and optionally add a moonstone. Place the bottle on your windowsill or porch where it can bask in the moonlight. Recite a prayer over it, such as this:

Grandmother Moon, with your comforting light,

Lend us your blessing and wisdom tonight.

As you dance with the sacred tides and flow,

Charge this holy water so I may help your blessings grow!

In the morning, collect your jar of holy water. Store in the refrigerator.

Blake Octavian Blair

NOTES:

March 2
Friday

3rd ♍

☽ v/c 6:50 pm

Color of the day: White
Incense of the day: Cypress

Day-After-Full Moon
Oceanic Bathtime

In many traditions of Witchcraft and other lunar-based spiritual paths, the day before and the day after the full moon (or new moon) are considered sacred because they jump-start the waxing or waning process. Today is the first day of lunar waning within the solar sign of Pisces, the intuitive water sign of the fishes.

Create an oceanic bath by drawing some warm water and adding sea salt, essential oils, seashells, and even pieces of nori (seaweed) if you dare! While you soak by candlelight, visualize the roaring sea, which is of course ruled by the tides of the moon. Consider playing some music, such as a CD featuring the sounds of the ocean.

Commune with the Great Goddess in her aspect of Mother Ocean. Allow the womb of life to take you within and provide you with cleansing from head to toe. Feel the Mother's warmth healing and protecting you from the inside out. Plug your nose and "scream" underwater to release pent-up energy. Finally, give thanks and visualize your stresses being released and flowing down the drain on this first day of the waning tide.

Raven Digitalis

Notes:

March 3
Saturday

3rd ♍

☽ → ♎ 3:20 am

Color of the day: Gray
Incense of the day: Ivy

My Magical Economy

The word *economy* comes from the Greek *oikonomia*, meaning "household management." Originally it meant far more than merely money, and included the division of labor, the management of resources, people, and time, and the way an entire household worked together to sustain one another.

Today, set up a "magical economy" altar. Gather the following items:

- A few coins (money)
- A watch or clock (time)
- A pay stub or job ad (work/occupation)
- A stone or stick (nature)
- A toy (play)
- A picture of your housemates, even if it's just you and your cat (relationships)

Place these on a pink cloth (representing love). In a fireproof stand, light a candle. Affirm:

I brighten my work, home, and life. I love all that I do.

I enjoy ample time, energy, love, and money.

I'm abundant and healthy, happy and wealthy.

I'm blessed by magical economy.

Repeat regularly as needed. What you choose to nurture will grow.

Dallas Jennifer Cobb

NOTES:

March 4
Sunday

3rd ♎

Color of the day: Gold
Incense of the day: Hyacinth

Pleasant Dreams with Primrose

As winter wanes and the first new green shoots of grass begin to rise, small pots of primroses begin to appear in garden centers and DIY stores everywhere. These pretty flowers lighten my heart, and I always buy some to fill flower boxes and to tuck around my garden.

Plant primroses in your garden to attract the fae and safeguard your property, or carry a pressed primrose blossom with you to ensure a safe journey.

Primroses have long been associated with children. According to folklore, placing the dried blossoms on children's bedding will ensure their respect for their elders.

Since primroses are also associated with protection and pleasant dreams, here is a spell to encourage sleep for your little one. Place a pot of bright primroses on the nightstand near your child's bed and have them say:

First rose of spring,

Pleasant dreams I seek,

And protection this night as I sleep.

Blessed be!

Monica Crosson

March 5
Monday

3rd ♎

☽ v/c 1:19 am

☽ → ♏ 8:23 am

Color of the day: Silver
Incense of the day: Lily

Spell for Getting Fit

Spring will be upon us soon, and we may find that our springtime clothes are, *ahem*, a little tighter than usual. Holiday indulgence and winter blahs can make us lose motivation to exercise, but a bit of work to renew our intentions can help us get back in gear. It's frustrating trying to lose weight when results seem to be so slow in coming. In addition to your chosen diet or fitness routine, try this spell to help see results.

Put on your workout gear (or whatever clothes you exercise in) and stand before a mirror. Look at yourself up and down, then look in your eyes and say:

I am getting fitter and
healthier every day.

Do this after you return from exercising (even walking the dog!) or after you've made healthy eating choices. Make sure you do it to observe any small milestone (an old pair of jeans fits again or you increase the mileage or the intensity of your workout), and do it at least once a day regardless of whether you have exercise planned. This will remind you that you're making a positive effort and continuing to make progress.

Peg Aloi

NOTES:

March 6
Tuesday

3rd ♏

Color of the day: Scarlet
Incense of the day: Geranium

Release an Old Flame

If things are over between you and an ex-partner, but they don't quite feel over in the energetic realm, it's time to cut the cords. First, if you have any of their old stuff, get it out of your space. Drop it by when they're not home or (if you've reasonably tried to return it and can't) donate it to a thrift store. Next, safely smudge your space with a bundle of desert sage. When this is complete, hold a modest length of hemp twine between your hands. Say:

> This cord represents all lingering attachments between me and (name of your ex-partner).

Snip the twine with scissors and then safely burn both halves: throw them in a fire or burn them in a cauldron or pot. Finally, smudge yourself with the sage and give thanks to the divine for cutting the cords, cleansing you of their residue, and allowing you to reclaim your power.

Tess Whitehurst

March 7
Wednesday

3rd ♏

☽ v/c 3:55 am
☽ → ♐ 5:03 pm

Color of the day: Topaz
Incense of the day: Bay laurel

Banishing the Garbage

Whether it's food scraps or personal items, people throw out a lot of garbage. Magically speaking, garbage is a connection to our lives and should be managed the same as any other. We must be just as mindful about what we release from our lives as we are about what we allow into them.

All the practical advice of shredding important documents applies of course, but it is also magically helpful to sever any ties we may have to what is tossed out, especially old clothes, nail clippings, etc. A quick and effective means of breaking the connection is to simply cast a banishing pentagram over the bag of garbage before you throw it out. Point at the bag and draw a pentagram (starting at the lower-left point and moving up to the center, then lower right, then upper left, then right, and back down) over the bag to release all ties, then toss it out.

Michael Furie

March 8
Thursday

3rd ✗

Color of the day: Purple
Incense of the day: Myrrh

Banish Negative Labels Spell

We've all experienced, at some time in our lives, the disappointment and anger of having someone try to tell us who we are. We might be called "lazy" by Mom or Dad, "stupid" by people at school, "overly sensitive" by former partners, or something even worse.

With the waning moon, the energies of holding on and letting go are highlighted, so take some old scrap paper (because labels are never worth our nice paper!) and write out as many erroneous labels as you can think of. Pin or tape the labels to yourself, then light a dark blue candle next to a fireproof dish. Pull the labels off, one by one. Read them aloud and banish them, saying *I am NOT _____!* as you burn the paper. Then, on nice paper, write down all the things you like about yourself. Whenever your thoughts turn to those old labels, replace them with the new affirmations of self-love, and be blessed.

Thuri Calafia

March 9
Friday

3rd ✗
4th Quarter 6:20 am
☽ v/c 9:27 pm

Color of the day: Coral
Incense of the day: Violet

Celebrate Success

By now, either you are set in a routine that incorporates your New Year's resolutions or you have given up on them entirely. Take time to celebrate your successes. Even an abandoned resolution isn't necessarily a bad thing. Maybe the resolution or the timing wasn't right for you.

We often expect the first day of January to give us a new perception of life, but a new year doesn't erase the past. Spend time meditating about the positive changes you have made in your life (all of them, not just those made since the beginning of the year). Celebrate these successes. YOU are capable of making changes for the better whenever you want and feel you are ready for it. Be your own cheerleader. Tell yourself you did a great job.

It's hard to be successful when focusing on failures. Focusing on our success makes future success more possible!

Kerri Connor

March 10
Saturday

4ᵗ⁴ ♐

☽ → ♑ 4:52 am

Color of the day: Blue
Incense of the day: Sage

Binding a Gossiper

If someone is spreading gossip or lies about you or others, and you've already tried to reason with this person, it's time to take magical action. Do this spell after you've already tried other approaches that haven't worked.

Set Kali and/or Ma'at on your altar and begin your visualization. See the gossiper busy spreading lies. Freeze him. Visualize getting out your magical purple duct tape. Tear off a piece and cover the gossiper's mouth. (Make sure he can still breathe.) Then tear off a long piece and wrap it around his face to keep his mouth from moving. Use more magical purple duct tape to tie the gossiper's hands and arms to his sides (so he can't reach up and pull the tape off). Tape his feet together so he can't walk.

Now give the gossiper an extended time-out by standing him in a corner. Do this visualization at dawn and at dusk for nine consecutive days.

Barbara Ardinger

 March 11
Sunday

4ᵗ⁴ ♑

Color of the day: Amber
Incense of the day: Eucalyptus

**Daylight Saving Time
begins at 2:00 a.m.**

Gathering the Sun

Daylight saving time was created to extend the daylight hours. On this day, gather the sun to you in order to increase your potential for success. Begin by gathering items that pertain to sun energies, such as sunstones, sunflowers, yellow or gold cloth, and gold jewelry. Once you have gathered the items you wish to use, place them together on your altar. Raise your arms up toward the sun and say:

I gather the energies of the sun to create success and my will be done.

Charlynn Walls

March 12
Monday

4th ♑

☽ v/c 11:36 am

☽ → ♒ 6:44 pm

Color of the day: White

Incense of the day: Narcissus

Sweep Winter Away Spell

This spell is based on an old German folk magic belief that you can sweep negative forces out of your home using a broom. In this case, we're going to sweep the remnants of winter out the door.

You'll need a broom and some salt. Begin by sprinkling a bit of salt along the threshold of all exterior doors. Then begin to sweep your home, moving toward all exterior doors. You may actually sweep or just use the gesture of sweeping. Visualize winter darkness being swept toward the exterior doors. Continue sweeping until you're just outside your threshold. At each threshold, sweep out the salt as you say:

Broom, sweep away winter from every crack and every spot,

Sweep away darkness, gloom, and all that rot!

Now that your home has had a psychic cleaning, you're ready for spring.

James Kambos

March 13
Tuesday

4th ♒

Color of the day: Red

Incense of the day: Cedar

Invoking Uranus

Surprise! Today Uranus was "discovered" by Sir William Herschel in 1781. Uranus, named for the Greek god Ouranos, is daddy to Cronos (Saturn) and granddaddy to Zeus (Jupiter), making him the real father in the sky. His 84-year orbit around the sun often brings change in his wake, sometimes unexpected.

Work with Uranus to restore your equilibrium when change has rocked your world. Visualize his blue-green glory, take his energy into your heart, and invoke his help:

Sky daddy,

Big daddy,

Master of surprise,

Shake me!

Wake me!

Open my eyes!

Repeat the incantation whenever a surprising shift happens in your life. Even if Uranus isn't behind it, he's got your back!

Natalie Zaman

March 14
Wednesday

4th ♒

Color of the day: Yellow
Incense of the day: Marjoram

Lucky Charms

Who couldn't use a bit more luck? This spell will help, but it's not a guarantee to fix your life! Success requires effort as well as magical intervention.

You'll need a piece of jewelry. It can be something that you already own but not something that you currently wear often. You'll also need a green candle and something to light it with. Light the candle and pass the piece of jewelry just above the flame. As you do so, recite these words:

Fire, fleet, and candlelight,

Lend an ear and hear my plight.

May your fortune smile on me

And bring me luck, so mote it be!

Now pinch out the flame and keep the candle somewhere safe. Wear the jewelry to remind you that the harder you work, the luckier you'll be. Repeat the spell with the same candle when an extra boost is needed.

Charlie Rainbow Wolf

March 15
Thursday

4th ♒

☽ v/c 3:32 am
☽ → ♓ 6:12 am

Color of the day: Turquoise
Incense of the day: Balsam

Grounding and Centering

These two techniques are an important part of all magic and spellwork, but they're often overlooked. Centering before spellcrafting will help your work be more effective. As for grounding, a failure to ground after magical workings can leave one tired, headachy, and even queasy—the so-called magic hangover. Let's prevent that from happening.

Think of centering as a kind of intense magical focus. Sit quietly, with eyes closed. Be aware of your own energy. Imagine it contracting into a soft ball somewhere around your midsection. Hold it there, feeling your energy focusing in that one spot. Open your eyes—you're ready to work.

Grounding is a way to dispose of excess or leftover energy. Sit on the ground (outdoors, if possible), with your back against a wall or tree and your hands on the ground. Imagine excess energy being siphoned through your body, into your hands, and down into the earth. Breathe deeply, taking as long as you need. It is done.

Susan Pesznecker

March 16

Friday

4℞ ♓

Color of the day: Pink
Incense of the day: Thyme

Romance Reboot

The timing is right to employ the water element to end old relationship problems and clear out patterns and programs that no longer serve. Draw a bath in a dark bathroom lit only by the light of a single pink candle, set next to a red rose and a piece of chocolate as a small offering to Aphrodite. Dissolve a full cup of sea salt in your bathwater, along with one-half cup Epsom salt and one tablespoon baking soda. Stand above the water and say:

> Aphrodite, I call on you. Please infuse this water with purification and love. May it cancel, clear, and delete all old problems, patterns, and programs related to relationships that no longer serve. May they dissolve into nothing and leave my heart happy, open, and free.

Soak in the water for at least forty minutes and give thanks to Aphrodite for supporting your cleanse.

Tess Whitehurst

 March 17

Saturday

4℞ ♓

☽ v/c 9:12 am
New Moon 9:12 am
☽ → ♈ 2:57 pm

Color of the day: Black
Incense of the day: Magnolia

Saint Patrick's Day

New Beginnings Spell

Have you ever heard the saying "Every new beginning comes from some other beginning's end"? Sometimes it's hard to let go of what's holding us back, even when we know it's what's best for us. What kind of new beginning are you looking at? A new job? Maybe a move to another city? How about letting go of a bad habit for a healthier you?

The new moon is the perfect time to embrace change! For this spell you will need a black candle, a seed, and a small terracotta pot with dirt.

Light the black candle to represent what you are releasing. It could be an unsatisfying job or an unhealthy lifestyle. Focus on letting go. Snuff out the candle, releasing your old life.

Take the seed and plant it in the pot. Focus on the growth of your new beginning. Visualize yourself healthier and happier. Say a few positive affirmations to close.

Monica Crosson

March 18

Sunday

1st ♈

Color of the day: Orange
Incense of the day: Juniper

Relationship Checkup

We often take our relationships for granted. The people we care for often know we do care about them, but how often do we really tell them and show them?

Today, take some paper (stationery would be great) and get ready for some actual letter writing—not email, but actual letters. You will also need a yellow candle and either juniper, myrrh, orange, or sandalwood oil. Pick the one you like best.

Light your candle and say:

Goddess, grant me the insight and knowledge to be open and loving.

Make a list of the people in your life who need to know they are loved and appreciated, the ones you don't tell often enough. Write them each a letter and then sprinkle a couple of drops of oil on the letter. Blow out the candle. Either hand-deliver the letters or actually mail them.

Kerri Connor

March 19

Monday

1st ♈

☽ v/c 3:29 pm

☽ → ♉ 9:07 pm

Color of the day: Gray
Incense of the day: Hyssop

Gratitude on Saint Joseph's Day

Today is Saint Joseph's Day, an anticipated occasion for celebration in Sicilian culture. The Sicilians create large altar-like tables of food called "Saint Joseph's tables," or *tavole di San Giuseppe*. These altar-esque tables are stacked to capacity with various kinds of delectable foods, but the star of this celebration is bread. The bread is baked into various artful shapes, such as baskets, fruits, suns, moons, animals, and even angels. The purpose of the celebration is to show gratitude for Saint Joseph's continued protection of the family and the bounty of food from the earth. The bread in both traditional Sicilian culture and modern Pagan culture remains a symbol of bounty.

Today, using a favorite recipe, bake your own bread in a shape that is meaningful to you as a symbol of your gratitude for the earth's bounty and for all that you have. Place the bread upon your altar to charge until you serve it at dinner.

Blake Octavian Blair

March 20
Tuesday

1st ♉

☉ → ♈ 12:15 pm

Color of the day: Maroon
Incense of the day: Cinnamon

Spring Equinox – Ostara

A Springtime Altar for the Equinox

Happy spring equinox! It's a special feeling to realize that daytime and nighttime exist in equilibrium for but a moment, and only twice a year. The energy of balance is all around us at this time, waiting for us to utilize it beneficially. Today, day and night are of equal length. In the Northern Hemisphere, we now begin our ascent into the light half of the year.

As a Neopagan archetype for the light half of the year, the Horned One has been known by numerous names over time and across cultures. What does this bright, wild, solar embodiment mean to you?

Today, take a nice long walk outside to find natural items that represent this archetypal force and the projective energy of the solar year. Perhaps you will find a bit of newly sprouted grass, a bud on a tree, a brightly colored stone, and so on. (Note: Be careful not to over-pick. Please pay attention to local regulations and use common sense.)

Arrange the items on your personal altar and focus on them every day until Midsummer to harness the growing energy of the conquering sun.

Raven Digitalis

NOTES:

March 21
Wednesday

1st ♉

☽ v/c 1:21 pm

Color of the day: Brown
Incense of the day: Honeysuckle

Spring Cleaning Spell

The beginning of spring is the perfect time for cleaning with intention! You're not just clearing cobwebs, dust, and grime, but clearing your home's stale energy and creating a fresh space to welcome in new energies of possibility, prosperity, and healing.

For this spell you will need ¼ cup salt and a teaspoon each of rosemary and lavender buds. For the essential oil spray you will need 3 to 4 drops of essential oil (fir, lemon, or orange are fine and smell great) for each 8 ounces of water.

Mix the salt, rosemary, and lavender buds together in a bowl, then sprinkle the mixture in all the corners of your rooms, working clockwise around the house from your starting point. Sweep or vacuum up the mixture, visualizing the removal and dispersal of all negative energy. Then spritz the corners of the rooms with the essential oil spray and invite in positive energy as you go, speaking your intentions aloud in whatever way is comfortable. You can use additional herbs or essential oils for specific intentions, such as cinnamon for money, lavender for healing, rose water for love, or basil for protection.

Peg Aloi

Notes:

March 22
Thursday

1st ♉

☽ → ♊ 1:30 am

Color of the day: Green
Incense of the day: Jasmine

Thor's Day

Named for the Norse god Thor, the protector of humankind, Thursday is a good day for a protection spell. Thor is the god of thunder, so why not use thunderous sound to clear your home? Sound waves help to rearrange and change latent energy patterns. The vacuum cleaner is perfect for this, loud and disruptive. It can break up energy and then suck it up and easily dispel it. It will also help with physical cleaning, removing dirt and dust.

The word *widdershins* comes from the Old High German *widar*, meaning "back" or "against," and *sinnen*, meaning "to travel." Move counterclockwise (widdershins) from room to room and within rooms as much as possible, quickly disturbing, transforming, removing, and dispelling stagnant energy. As you clutch the vacuum, envision Thor wielding his hammer. Channel his strength and protection and let his rumbling thunder chase away negative energy, worry, or fear. Empty the vacuum outdoors when you're finished.

Dallas Jennifer Cobb

March 23
Friday

1st ♊

☽ v/c 11:52 pm

Color of the day: White
Incense of the day: Vanilla

Fairy Love Spell

To draw a new love, find red primroses at your local nursery and pot them. If weather permits, place them near your front or back door. Touch the pot with both hands, gaze lovingly at the flowers, and say:

Flower of love, realm of the fey,
bring me a lover before it is May.

Today and every following Friday until the spell has done its job, place one shiny dime in the pot and then kindly and gently snip one blossom. Slip it into a small muslin bag and pin it inside your clothes near your heart. As you do so, feel the feelings associated with the love you'd like to attract. Devotedly tend to the living flowers as long as they flourish. When your spell has succeeded, share a bottle of champagne with your new love after offering the first glass to the earth in gratitude to the fairies.

Tess Whitehurst

March 24
Saturday

1st ♍ ♊

☽ → ♋ 4:53 am

2nd Quarter 11:35 am

Color of the day: Indigo
Incense of the day: Pine

Overcoming Obstacles to Success

Since this day has both the first quarter moon and Mercury in retrograde, it's an excellent time to overcome obstacles, "turning a corner" to greater success.

For this spell, create an oil from 1 tablespoon oregano, 1 tablespoon mint, and ¼ cup almond (or sunflower) oil. Set a cauldron in the middle of an altar table, with a white candle to its left and an orange candle to the right. On a piece of paper, write the obstacle to overcome in black ink. Anoint both candles with the oil you've made and light them, left then right.

Hold the paper, focusing on overcoming this problem, then light it in the flames of the white and then the orange candle, saying:

Mercury moving through the past,
sun squared moon, adds to the charm;
to overcome obstacles, fortune at last,
victory gained, free from harm.

Drop the paper into the cauldron to burn to ashes.

Michael Furie

March 25
Sunday

2nd ♋

Color of the day: Gold
Incense of the day: Frankincense

Palm Sunday

Candle and the Wind

Today is Sir Elton John's birthday, and like him, you can break bad habits and rise to personal success. You'll need a white candle and a match, pen and paper, and a white candle. It's best to do this outside, but inside will also work.

Light the candle. Using the pen and paper, write down the habit you want to break. Fold the paper four times. With each fold, repeat a line of this verse:

By fold of four, open the door.

By fold of three, so mote it be.

By fold of two, the spell is true.

By fold of one, this vice is gone.

Put the paper on a heatproof surface. Set it on fire and let it burn away, ashes to the wind. (If you do this inside, save the ashes and take them outside to the wind when you can.) Pinch out the candle and trust the process.

Charlie Rainbow Wolf

March 26
Monday

2nd ♋

☽ v/c 2:58 am

☽ → ♌ 7:45 am

Color of the day: Lavender
Incense of the day: Clary sage

Friendship Spell

Ever feel like your friends aren't what you're looking for? Often we sell ourselves short, thinking we don't deserve the kind of support and kindness we give others. It's time to fix our broken pickers and boost the quality of our friendships!

First, choose a small crystal—a cluster with points going in several directions is best. Then, at your altar, make a list of all the things you seek in high-quality friends, and notice how like your own gifts these things are. Let yourself bask in the glow of those feelings for a moment, telling yourself that you deserve the best! Now visualize light pouring forth from the crystal points up into the sky like a myriad of searchlights. Say:

I'm sending up a beacon to pierce the darkest night. Come see how awesome I can be! Behold my shining light!

Chant this until the crystal is saturated with your positive energy, and wear it on your person in social situations.

Thuri Calafia

March 27
Tuesday

2nd ♌

Color of the day: Black
Incense of the day: Basil

What Are You Thinking About?

Our minds are going all the time. But what's going on in there? What are you currently reading? Books? Social media? What's bothering you? What do you need to learn?

Set Athena or another god or goddess of wisdom on your altar and cast your circle. Speak these words:

Holy powers of wisdom, goddesses and gods of mental power,

I seek intellectual understanding.

I seek to know _____.

Holy powers of intellectual understanding,

Come into my life, touch my every step,

Bless me with your gifts

Of reason, judgment, and discrimination.

Give me the gifts

Of fresh air, of new ideas, of clarity of thought and speech.

Great and generous powers,

I need to understand _____.

Barbara Ardinger

March 28
Wednesday

2nd ♌

☽ v/c 5:54 am

☽ → ♍ 10:30 am

Color of the day: Yellow
Incense of the day: Lilac

Spell for Keeping a Loved One Close

Today's waxing moon is ideal for this spell.

Light a silver or white candle. Meditate on your loved one, imagining them close to you.

Cut a six-inch circle from pink or red cloth. Within the circle, place a small photo of your loved one and, if possible, a little snippet of their hair (to boost the sympathetic magic). Add small items or mementos that symbolize your relationship. You might add a few rose, daisy, or lavender petals. Use a cord to tie the circle shut hobo-style, closing it with a square knot.

Light a second silver (or white) candle and set the bundle between the two candles. Repeat:

As these candles burn so brightly,

Bridge the gap twixt you and me.

Whether your absence be short or long,

Keep our souls' connection strong.

Extinguish the candles and place them on your altar. Keep the bundle close to you.

Susan Pesznecker

 March 29
Thursday

2nd ♍

Color of the day: Crimson
Incense of the day: Nutmeg

Removing Illusions

Today is Smoke and Mirrors Day, which typically honors that which is associated with magicians and that which is unseen. As magickal practitioners, we can work with this concept to remove illusions that are creating a blockage for us.

Take a small mirror and cover it with a square of cloth. Focus on your intention to remove the illusions that are keeping you from seeing the truth of a situation. As you do so, slowly remove the square of cloth from the mirror. Once the cloth is removed, you will be able to see in the mirror and the illusion will be removed, revealing what lies underneath.

Charlynn Walls

March 30
Friday

2nd ♏

☽ v/c 12:59 am

☽ → ♎ 1:52 pm

Color of the day: Rose
Incense of the day: Orchid

Good Friday

A Growth Spell to Persephone

Persephone is the ancient Greek goddess of spring. She spends six months of the year with the god Hades as goddess of the underworld and six months on Earth with her mother, Demeter. Her arrival on Earth is marked by the beginning of spring. You can use this spell to achieve growth in any area of your life, such as career, finances, or your personal life. To begin, write your wish with metallic gold ink on paper, then say:

> Persephone, goddess of
> spring, thank you
>
> For the green earth and for
> the flowers in the meadow.
>
> Grant my wish and help it grow.

Hide the wish. Then at Mabon, when Persephone is about to return to the underworld, burn the wish and scatter the ashes outside.

James Kambos

 ## March 31
Saturday

2nd ♎

Full Moon 8:37 am

Color of the day: Blue
Incense of the day: Patchouli

Passover begins

Full Moon Wishing Stones

When Luna is in her full phase, she brings us some of her most potent energies for fulfillment—perfect for wish granting! Bring her power down to earth to keep with you for the next month. You'll need thirty white and/or gray stones of any kind. Go outside (to a spot where the moonlight will touch the stones, if possible) and arrange them in a solid circle. Leave them out overnight to absorb the moon's energy with a blessing:

> Mirror, mirror, on the ground,
>
> Luna smiles when she looks down.
>
> Wane to new, wax full again,
>
> To these tokens your energies send.

Over the course of the next lunar cycle, use a stone a day to make a wish or simply bring full moon energy to your daily routine. At the end of each day, place the stone in a bowl of saltwater to cleanse it for the next full moon cycle.

Natalie Zaman

April

This month we move from dark to light, from cold to warm, from brown to green. April is a magical month that starts with April Fools' Day and ends on the eve of May Day, begins with a joke and ends with an outdoor sleep-out. Here in Ontario, Canada, the average temperature at the beginning of April is close to freezing. It's common to have snow on the ground. Throughout April a magical transformation occurs: the temperature climbs as high as 66 degrees Fahrenheit (19 degrees Celsius) and flowers bloom.

Post-equinox, the days grow longer. Between April 1 and 30, the daylight increases from 12 hours and 46 minutes to 14 hours and 8 minutes. As the sun travels northward, it climbs in the sky. Not only do days lengthen, but shadows shorten as well. It is inviting to get outdoors. Like the plants that need sunlight to conduct photosynthesis, we humans need sunlight to help manufacture vitamin D.

This month, make time to enjoy the outdoors. Get out in the daylight, take evening walks in the twilight after dinner, contemplate your garden, and turn your face toward the sun at every chance. With winter coming to an end, now is your time to transform.

Dallas Jennifer Cobb

April 1
Sunday

3rd ♎︎

☽ v/c 2:29 pm

☽ → ♏︎ 6:57 pm

Color of the day: Amber
Incense of the day: Almond

April Fools' Day –
All Fools' Day – Easter

No More the Fool

This spell works with the Fool card in the tarot. If you don't have your own tarot deck, print a copy of this card from an image online. The Fool is pure and innocent, and this ritual takes you back to a time when life was less complicated, before you started thinking you needed to be someone, before other people's opinions influenced how you thought you should live your life.

Put the card in a place where you'll see it frequently. You could put it on your fridge or make it your screen saver, for example. Every time you see the card, repeat to yourself this old rhyme:

Sticks and stones may break my bones but words will never hurt me.

Let that be a reminder to you that other people's opinions are just that: opinions, not facts. Celebrate your uniqueness, and let it lead you to the life you were meant to live.

Charlie Rainbow Wolf

April 2
Monday

3rd ♏︎

Color of the day: Ivory
Incense of the day: Rosemary

A home and Garden Protection Spell

The earthy scents of spring fill the air now. This is a good time to protect your home and garden with this spell. You'll need a few drops of olive oil, a hoe, and some lettuce seed. If you don't have a garden, you may perform this spell using a window box or flowerpot.

First, bless the garden by sprinkling a few drops of olive oil on the soil. Next, using the hoe (if you have a garden), loosen the soil. Then using the hoe or your finger, trace the shape of a pentagram or other holy symbol into the soil. Now plant the lettuce seed. Lettuce has powerful protective qualities that will protect the home and garden, and lettuce should grow well for you during the cooler spring weather. Lastly, give a silent thanks to Mother Earth for providing us with food.

James Kambos

April 3
Tuesday

3rd ♏

☽ v/c 12:06 pm

Color of the day: White
Incense of the day: Ylang-ylang

Tree Awakening

You can connect with the spirit of a tree during the spring by working to fully awaken the tree. Pick a time of day when it will be quiet so you can connect fully with the tree and hear what it has to say. To do so, you will want to be able to physically touch the tree. Reach out your hands and touch the roots and the trunk. Take a deep breath and connect to the root system. Feel it bring the nutrients up into the trunk. If there is a blockage, try to work with the tree to remove it so that it can awaken fully. When things are flowing smoothly and you can feel that the tree has awoken, you can listen to the wisdom that it has to offer. Connect with the tree often and bring it small offerings throughout the year.

Charlynn Walls

April 4
Wednesday

3rd ♏

☽ → ♐ 2:55 am

Color of the day: Topaz
Incense of the day: Marjoram

Benedict the Moor

Today is the Catholic feast day of Saint Benedict the Moor, or Saint Benedict the Black. The child of slaves from Ethiopia who were living in Sicily, he gained his freedom at eighteen and went on to perform many miracles, including healing the sick. He was also a natural clairvoyant and claircognizant and was said to enjoy cooking.

Light a white candle to Saint Benedict today and offer him a snifter or small bottle of brandy. If you'd like, place these near a small picture of him and/or an image of a flaming heart. Request that he support you in initiating or deepening your intuitive and healing abilities. If protection from infectious diseases is a magical intention of yours, you might petition him for this purpose as well. Additionally, he can be petitioned for the promotion of social justice and racial equality as well as the eradication of slavery.

Tess Whitehurst

April 5

Thursday

3rd ♐

Color of the day: Purple
Incense of the day: Apricot

honoring the Ancestors

Today marks the date of the Taiwanese holiday Qing Ming Jie. This holiday is also known as Tomb-Sweeping Day. The Taiwanese people are very diligent about maintaining their loved ones' graves. Sweeping, cleaning, and picking up around the graves and replacing decorations, flowers, and offerings are some of the main activities on this day. You can do the same today at a loved one's gravesite, or you can honor your ancestors at home.

If you choose to honor your ancestors at home, create a simple ancestor altar upon a cloth in a clean space, perhaps with photos and mementos. Offer your departed loved ones food and drink and perhaps a candle and fresh flowers. State your prayers to them at the altar and include them in spirit during your activities throughout the day. Remember, ancestors of blood and spirit are always there to call upon.

Blake Octavian Blair

April 6

Friday

3rd ♐
☽ v/c 9:36 am
☽ → ♑ 2:01 pm

Color of the day: Pink
Incense of the day: Alder

Pillar of Salt

A circle of salt has long acted as a protective barrier and delineator of sacred space. On this day in 1930, Mahatma Gandhi stood at the edge of the Arabian Sea, picked up a lump of mud and salt, and said, "With this, I am shaking the foundations of the British Empire."

Stand in a quiet space that is sacred to you, and use salt to draw a circle around yourself. Inside the circle's protective embrace, take a moment to ground and center. Visualize whatever it is you need to overcome, then take a fistful of salt in each hand, raise your arms over your head, and say:

With this salt, I shake the
foundations of (insert your issue)!

Place your clenched fists over your heart, step out of the circle, and go outdoors. Picture that which you need to conquer once more, then throw the salt at it and watch it dissolve.

Natalie Zaman

April 7
Saturday

3rd ♑

Color of the day: Gray
Incense of the day: Sandalwood

Passover ends

Clootie Magic

The tradition of clooties dates back to well dressing, an old Irish/Scottish/English custom. Wells and springs, regarded as sacred for their life-giving properties, were "dressed" with colored stones, gems, flowers, and small structures.

A clootie is a cloth strip that was dipped in the water and tied to a tree near the well. As the clootie was tied, prayer was made to the nature spirits or deities known to favor the area. Clooties could also represent ailments; as the clootie disintegrated, it carried sickness away with it.

You can work your own clootie magic. Identify a tree in your own yard, ideally one near water. Cut long strips of natural fiber cloth (natural fibers biodegrade safely). Write wishes or petitions on the strips or just envision your wishes as you tie the clooties to the tree. Leave the clooties in place until they disintegrate naturally, at which time your wish should be realized.

Susan Pesznecker

April 8
Sunday

3rd ♑
4th Quarter 3:18 am
☽ v/c 10:40 pm

Color of the day: Yellow
Incense of the day: Heliotrope

Turn Your Home into a Shrine

Generally defined, a shrine is where a deity lives. You can turn your home into a shrine in which live not only gods and goddesses but also your family and your pets.

Invoke the elemental powers of each direction and ask them to bless your home. Find real, physical symbols. In the east, use symbols of elemental air: birds, bees, etc. Hang pictures on your eastern wall or set little birds or bees on a table or bookcase. In the south, use symbols of elemental fire: the sun, volcanic rocks, red or orange glass or stones, etc. In the west, use symbols of water: shells, mermaids, etc. In the north, use symbols of earth: beautiful rocks, green plants, etc. You can do this for your entire home or for each individual room.

If it's practical, set up a permanent altar in the center of your home. Invoke Hestia and ask her to be present in your home.

Barbara Ardinger

April 9
Monday

4th ♑

☽ → ♒ 2:50 am

Color of the day: Gray
Incense of the day: Neroli

healing Spell for father Sky

With air pollution and global warming becoming such an issue these days, it's even more vital that we, as practitioners of magic, do our part to help. Becoming involved in US Forest Service tree-planting efforts or even simply planting a seedling in a yard or in the wild (make sure it's of an indigenous species, however—nothing invasive that would upset the local ecosystems) can do much to help heal our ailing planet.

For this spell, you will need one (or several!) young trees and a green and a pink candle. Light the green candle, to honor the breath of the tree, and the pink one, to honor the breath of humans. Hold the baby tree while concentrating on exchanging your breath with that of the seedling, letting the energy flow between you. Chant:

*Life-giving tree, may we rise
together, healing and blessing
our beloved sky father.*

When the power peaks, send the energy into the sapling, visualizing it fully grown and healthy.

Thuri Calafia

April 10
Tuesday

4th ♒

Color of the day: Maroon
Incense of the day: Bayberry

Rainy Weather Attunement

Spring has sprung perhaps, but endless days of rain can make us feel drained and blue. On a rainy day in April, try observing the weather and shifting your perspective.

Look out your window and notice as much as you can. Is it raining softly or is it pouring? Is it dark and cloudy or is there sunlight breaking through the clouds? Is it cold and windy? Now open your front door and smell the air, and put your hand out to feel the rain. Open yourself to this moment, attune your senses, and let the weather's power affect you; feel how it changes from moment to moment.

As you go through your day, take note of your moods and energy, how they change like weather, too. You can use this mode of attunement with other kinds of weather as well, and heighten your sensitivity and awareness.

Peg Aloi

 ## April 11
Wednesday

4th ♒

☽ v/c 10:55 am
☽ → ♓ 2:40 pm

Color of the day: White
Incense of the day: Lavender

Whisking Away the Mental Cobwebs

In spring, the active power of air has prominence and can be utilized to enhance our mental powers, freeing our minds from clutter and distractions. For this spell, you have two options: you can stand outside on a breezy day (ideally) or use a portable fan placed in front of you set on low. Feel the air as it touches your skin. Connect with this element, visualizing that it's traveling through you. Breathe in and out gently. As you do, feel as though you're taking in the air through every pore of your body. In your mind's eye, see the flowing air sweeping away any blocks, confusion, or distractions as if they were puffs of smoke scattered on the breeze. When you feel ready, say:

From mental clutter I am now free,
as power of air moves through me;
clouded, vague thoughts are released,
new fresh focus, my mind at peace!

Michael Furie

April 12
Thursday

4th ♓

Color of the day: Green
Incense of the day: Carnation

Altar Reset

Altars are just as different from each other as the people who set them up. Some people have several altars—some for daily use, some for sabbat use, some for esbats, some for spells. Some people use the same altar and just change the setup to suit their needs at the time.

Spend some time today evaluating your altar. What do you like about it? Is there something you want to change? Are you too used to it, so that your practice has become monotonous? If you have been using the same setup for a long time, is there something you can add to it or change to update it?

Make any changes you want and spice up your altar. Breathe new life into it. Then do a brief altar cleansing (physical and spiritual), blessing, and dedication.

Kerri Connor

April 13
Friday

4th ♓

☽ v/c 7:27 am
☽ → ♈ 11:25 pm

Color of the day: Coral
Incense of the day: Mint

Early Preparation for Autumnal Abundance

Although autumn is two entire seasons away, it's fun to plan ahead and send energy toward future manifestations. Being springtime, it's time to sow the seeds for the coming autumnal harvest, both literally and figuratively! Contemplate the ways in which you can sow energetic seeds, such as new ways of thinking or projects you have in mind, which can take root and provide a "harvest" later in the year.

In addition to making solid plans for how abundance will manifest in the fall—which may also include gardening, crafting, art, or business-related goals—create a spell by growing wheatgrass indoors. Wheatgrass can be grown inside at any time of the year, and is a common component of juicing drinks and various health foods.

Upon procuring some wheatgrass seeds and growing instructions, plant the seeds and declare:

I sow these seeds of abundance to be reaped in the glory of the autumn!

When the sprouts pop up, visualize them helping grow your own manifestations. Tend to them daily and use the grass in your own manifestation magick—and food!

Raven Digitalis

NOTES:

April 14
Saturday

4th ♈

Color of the day: Brown
Incense of the day: Rue

Sweep Away Negativity with Nettle

Stinging nettle is one of the earliest spring greens and is native to Asia, Europe, and North America. The blanched tips are an excellent addition to pesto, and the dried leaves can be used to make a wonderful nutrition-packed tea that enhances psychic awareness.

An herb of protection since ancient times, nettle can be sprinkled around your home to protect your property, and a nettle leaf worn in your shoe is said to keep you from being led astray by evil.

Before your next ritual, add a few branches of stinging nettle to your besom to sweep away negativity from your ritual space.

A week before your ritual, use a pair of scissors to snip some branches of stinging nettle and hang to dry (remember to wear gloves—nettle stings!).

The evening before the ritual, use twine to tie some dry nettle onto your besom. After use, cut the nettle from the besom and add to the compost.

Monica Crosson

April 15

Sunday

4th ♈

New Moon 9:57 pm

Color of the day: Orange
Incense of the day: Hyacinth

Intention Setting

It's time to set an intention, planting a seed that will sprout and grow with the waxing moon. Today's new moon occurs in Aries, the first sign of the zodiac, providing an extra-powerful "fresh start" energy. Aries represents the personal, the "me" energy, so set a personal intention that will bear fruit at the next full moon (on April 29th). Meditate on your intention. Write it down, worded positively (avoid negative descriptions). Here are some examples:

I complete a rough draft of the article.
I enjoy radiant energy.
I'm focused and successful at work.
I'm happy.

Now fold the paper in half, envisioning your intention growing. Fold it again and see your success. Picture the fruits of your intention, and fold the paper as many times as you can, concentrating the intention's energy. Over the next two weeks, do what is needed to water and nourish your intention, and look for success at the full moon.

Dallas Jennifer Cobb

 April 16

Monday

1st ♈

☽ v/c 1:59 am

☽ → ♉ 4:51 am

Color of the day: White
Incense of the day: Narcissus

Offering Blessings

As a magical person, you may be in a situation to give blessings to others (or you may wish to bless yourself).

If possible, work at or near sunrise or at high noon.

Place the person to be blessed in the east and stand facing them. Make physical contact with them in one or more of these ways: by taking one or both of their hands, by placing one hand on one of their shoulders, and/or by placing one hand on their head.

Repeat the following:

To the universe [or substitute a deity name, if desired]:

I entreat you to protect your servant (name of person to be blessed).

Keep him/her safe from harm and wrongdoing.

Guide him/her with certainty to the right path.

Bless his/her days with love, light, and warmth.

So may it be!

You might also include smudging in the blessing ceremony. Blue or white candles would add to the blessing, as would the use of clear quartz.

Susan Pesznecker

NOTES:

 April 17
Tuesday

1st ♉

☽ v/c 6:05 pm

Color of the day: Scarlet
Incense of the day: Ginger

Victory

There are many times when we are faced with a situation in which we could use a win. Victory provides a boost to our confidence and helps us when we face more difficult situations.

You can call on Mars to help provide victory in obtaining the perfect job for you. When interviewing for a new position, wear red and black, the colors of Mars, to aid in your victory. Call upon Mars when you are about to enter the interview, saying:

*Success is not a mystery, with
you aiding me in this victory.*

Charlynn Walls

April 18

Wednesday

1st ♉

☽ → ♊ 8:02 am

Color of the day: Brown
Incense of the day: Bay laurel

Carry Me Tarot Meditation

Life is full of journeys—and not just the kind where you jump in a car, plane, or train and go on an adventure. Challenges, even the day-to-day sort, are journeys that carry us to (hopefully!) higher destinations. Sometimes these trips are hard. Use this tarot meditation to get over the most challenging of challenges.

You will need the Six of Swords, the Eight of Cups, and the Chariot. As you lay out each tarot card, visualize your particular issue and relate it to the images on the card. Then speak the incantation for the card aloud, as follows:

Six of Swords (representing where you are now):

I have moved on from rough waters.

Eight of Cups (representing where you are going):

I rise above it. There's no turning back.

Chariot (representing your attitude):

I am in the driver's seat.

Repeat this meditation each time you embark on a challenging journey of any kind.

Natalie Zaman

 April 19

Thursday

1st ♊

☉ → ♉ 11:13 pm

Color of the day: Crimson
Incense of the day: Myrrh

A Flower and Garlic Spell for the home

Spring flowers, such as lilacs or white tulips, team up with garlic in this spell to remove any negative vibrations from the home.

First, place a bouquet of lilacs, white tulips, or flowers of your choice in the center of your home. On a paper plate, place three cloves of garlic that have been sliced, and cover them with salt. To protect the table surface, put a piece of foil next to the flowers, then set the plate of garlic and salt on the foil. Leave undisturbed overnight.

The next morning, without touching the garlic or salt, put the foil, plate, garlic, and salt in a plastic bag. Tie it shut and toss it in the trash. When the flowers fade, compost them. Your home is now free of any negativity.

James Kambos

April 20
Friday

1st ♊

☽ v/c 8:05 am

☽ → ♋ 10:26 am

Color of the day: Rose
Incense of the day: Orchid

Doing Good Works

When the headlines are just too overwhelming—too many homeless people, too many hungry children, too much violence, too much suffering and pain—we can turn to mother goddesses. We can find small ways to help other people.

Set Isis or Hera or another mother goddess on your altar. Cast your circle and say these words:

*Goddesses and gods of
the manifest world,*

*I seek understanding of the purpose
of good works and charity.*

*I want to know what I can do to
help _____.*

*Holy powers of practical
understanding,*

*Come into my life and
guide my every step.*

*Bless me with your gifts of
groundedness and abundance.*

Great and generous powers,

I want to help.

I need to take what action I can.

*Lead me on the path of
simple good works.*

Barbara Ardinger

Notes:

April 21
Saturday

1st ♋

Color of the day: Blue
Incense of the day: Ivy

Sacred Sexuality Spell

With Beltane coming, it's a good idea to focus on how we feel about love and sex, and to nurture those energies. Take some time to meditate on what is true for you, whether it's celibacy, wild orgies, or something in between. Know that it is your truth, and so long as you harm none in your fantasies or practices, no one can tell you that it's wrong. Harming none, of course, means that we don't cast spells on specific people, unless we have prior permission.

Once you're clear about what you truly desire, break up a rose or two into a clear glass bowl, and chant:

*Come to me, love, on the
whispering wind,*

*On the rays of the sun and
the roar of the sea.*

Come to me now, by the steadfast earth

And all the power of three times three.

Say this chant nine times, adding these last two lines at the end:

This spell is now sealed.

So mote it be.

You may wish to pleasure yourself while doing so, holding off on orgasm and letting the energy peak into the flower petals instead. Once you earth the power afterward, release the petals to the four directions and stand ready for your passion to manifest!

Thuri Calafia

NOTES:

April 22
Sunday

1st ♋

☽ v/c 10:58 am

☽ → ♌ 1:09 pm

2nd Quarter 5:46 pm

Color of the day: Gold
Incense of the day: Marigold

Earth Day

The Bees and Butterflies

On this Earth Day (which also falls on a first quarter moon), we can help to turn a corner on the worldwide imbalance of the insect populations, particularly the bees and the butterflies. Find or make an image or a figure of a bee and one of a butterfly. On an altar, place a gold candle on the left, then the bee image, a brown candle in the center, then the butterfly image, and a green candle to the right. Light the candles left to right to charge the images, saying:

Golden light of energy and power,
balance restored, blessing unleashed;
cycle renewed for insect and flower,
heal the earth, butterfly and bee;
increase in strength hour by hour,
for good of all, the magic set free.

Extinguish the candles and place the images where sunlight will fall on them and you'll see them often. This helps to release the magic.

Michael Furie

 April 23
Monday

2nd ♌

Color of the day: Silver
Incense of the day: Hyssop

Moonstone Spell for Divination

Mondays vibrate with lovely lunar energy that is perfect for enhancing divination and intuition. Who wouldn't want to harness a little bit of that to charge and give a boost to their divination tools? I like to store my divination tools with crystals, and here is a spell to give them some extra oomph!

Take a piece of moonstone and hold it between your hands. Repeat the following:

Moonstone, with your lunar hue,

Her intuitive energies I
intend to imbue,

Bask in and absorb on this Monday

Intuition and guidance, as you may.

Assist in charging my divining tools,

Guiding me along the way.

Now focus on your intent and touch the stone to your heart and then to your third eye. Now put the stone in your hands and blow your intent into it. Allow the stone to charge for the day on your altar, then store it with your divination tools.

Blake Octavian Blair

April 24
Tuesday

2nd ♌

☽ v/c 2:40 pm

☽ → ♍ 4:40 pm

Color of the day: Red
Incense of the day: Cedar

Abounding Spring

Spring bounded in weeks ago, and by now, its presence can be felt everywhere. Spend some time today outside reveling in the spring air. You will need a feather and a stick of incense (something floral or "springy") or a lavender smudge stick.

Light the incense or smudge stick and hold it in one hand. Take the feather in the other hand and use it to control and waft the smoke through the air. Dance around and have fun. Play some springy or lighthearted music. As you dance, feel the air all around you. Let it caress your skin. Feel it in your hair. Feel it fill your lungs with joy as you breathe deeply. Pause at times to close your eyes and let yourself feel everything around you. Give thanks for the refreshing, cleansing, renewing air.

Kerri Connor

April 25
Wednesday

2nd ♍

Color of the day: Yellow
Incense of the day: Lilac

Spring Garden Blessing

As the April sun begins to warm the earth, many of us can be found in our gardens planting seeds and weeding beds. This is a great time to bless your newly upturned plot of earth.

For this blessing we will be invoking Aine, a Celtic solar/lunar goddess and faerie queen. Aine was thought to have birthed the first sheaves of grain in Ireland, and agricultural rites are still practiced in her name.

For this blessing you will need a blue or green tealight candle, a flat stone, and a dish of water.

On a bright sunny morning, go into your garden and light your tealight on a flat stone. Dip your fingers into the water, and as you sprinkle the ground with it, say:

Aine, lady of light,

Bless this garden, bless this soil.

Bless our hands as they toil.

Bless the land with rain and sun

*And a bountiful harvest
when the season's done.*

Leave the tealight to burn out.

Monica Crosson

April 26
Thursday

2nd ♏

☽ v/c 5:49 am

☽ → ♎ 9:13 pm

Color of the day: Turquoise
Incense of the day: Mulberry

A Third-Eye Anointing for Visionary Slumber

The term *tilak* or *tilaka* refers to the holy marks worn by swamis and other members of Hinduism and related Eastern paths. Many adherents wear these markings on the third eye (brow) following meditation, yoga, and worship in the home and temple. These markings vary depending on one's sect and are often created by the use of vibhuti ash, kumkum, chandan (sandalwood) paste, and a variety of other powders. The modern bejeweled bindi sticker is related, being worn on the third eye (ajna chakra) of Indian brides—and often as everyday fashion!

To inspire visionary dreams, try a variation of tilak before sleep. After performing your own meditation and spiritual worship, anoint your third eye with any of the aforementioned substances or with a powdered herb such as turmeric, lavender, sage, saffron, or even powdered rice.

As you drift off to sleep, repeat this spell verbally and mentally:

Mystic spirits, sleeping mind,
grant me vision unconfined.

Raven Digitalis

NOTES:

April 27

Friday

2nd ♎

Color of the day: White
Incense of the day: Rose

Flower Magic

Floralia, the ancient Roman festival dedicated to the goddess Flora, was traditionally held from late April to early May, to celebrate the beauty and usefulness of plants and nature's eternal cycle of growth. What a perfect time to celebrate beauty!

To honor Flora, place a vase of freshly cut flowers on your altar (even better if they are spring flowers in bloom, like daffodils, hyacinths, or tulips). Get some annual flower seeds for summer flowers (like marigolds, zinnias, calendulas, or cosmos) and plant them in a pot, visualizing bringing beauty and vitality into your life. Water them regularly, keep them in a sunny window, and when the seedlings get two inches high, carefully transplant them outside.

When the flowers bloom, you may choose to enjoy them where they are, or pick a few and enjoy them in a vase. Be sure to put a few on your altar to enhance your magical workings.

Peg Aloi

April 28

Saturday

2nd ♎

Color of the day: Indigo
Incense of the day: Magnolia

Abundance Spell

The ancient Roman festival of Floralia used to run from today until May 3. It was a celebration of Flora, goddess of flowers, vegetation, and fertility. Having some association with May Day, Floralia is a day for fertile energy, whether you want to conceive a baby, make art, plant a garden, or sow success.

Go outside and stand with your feet wide apart. Envision the fertile energy of the awakening earth deep below. Inhale, drawing that energy up into your feet, then up your legs, through your sex organs, belly, spine, heart, and brain, and into your head. Now exhale, releasing the energy from the top of your head (crown chakra) and letting it cascade out and around you, returning to the ground. Do this several times, until you feel the results of the energy within you. Now take this energy and get to work in whatever area of your life will most benefit from the flowers of your fertile energy.

Dallas Jennifer Cobb

April 29

Sunday

2nd ♎︎

☽ v/c 1:32 am

☽ → ♏︎ 3:11 am

Full Moon 8:58 pm

Color of the day: Orange
Incense of the day: Eucalyptus

International Dance Day

Today is International Dance Day. Integral to every culture, dancing performs many functions in the social and sacred realms. For example, so many of us adore dancing under the full moon! Especially on a lunar power day like today, dancing can be employed to transform moods, situations, perspectives, and energy patterns.

So choose an energy pattern you'd like to shift or a condition you'd like to draw in. Light a red candle. Put on some music that makes your body want to move. Sit comfortably on the floor (or a chair, if necessary) and connect with your root chakra: the place where your body meets the earth. Breathe into this area until your body begins to merge with the music. Dance for at least ten minutes, knowing all the while that you are changing your frequency to match that which you'd like to draw in.

Tess Whitehurst

April 30

Monday

3rd ♏︎

☽ v/c 10:56 pm

Color of the day: Gray
Incense of the day: Lily

A Witch Jar for Protection

It's very easy to make a simple Witch jar if you're feeling vulnerable or you're worried that negative energy might come knocking on your door. You'll need the following:

- A glass jar with a tight lid
- Rusty old nails
- Shards of broken glass
- Old razor blades or pins— anything sharp (handle with care)
- Some vinegar
- A black candle
- Red string or ribbon

Fill the jar with the sharp objects, and pour the vinegar onto them. If you aren't squeamish and really want to be authentic, you can omit the vinegar and urinate in the jar! Place the lid on tightly. Light the black candle and let the wax drip around the seal, then tie it shut with the red ribbon. Bury the jar in front of the main doorway of your home, and it will trap negative energy before it enters the house.

Charlie Rainbow Wolf

Welcome to the famously merry month of May! Though it was originally named after the Greek fertility goddess Maia, the Catholic Church has since designated this month as sacred to the Virgin Mary, even referring to her as "the Queen of May" during this time. Day one of this flower-filled month is the beloved holiday of Beltane, during which the veil that usually conceals the world of the fairies fades, and our power to make contact with them reaches its yearly peak. Indeed, May's birth flower is a fairy favorite: the lily of the valley. As for our skies, this month they host the Eta Aquariids meteor shower, which reaches its peak around May 6 and is most visible before the sunrise.

May is also the month when the light half of the year begins to assert itself in earnest, and we sense the days lengthening, the sun growing warmer, and the leaves filling out the trees. This allows us to gaze bravely into our own brilliance and to courageously release anything that has been holding us back from being our most radiant, expansive, beautiful selves. Indeed, May's bright presence reminds us to claim the vital prosperity that is our birthright and our natural state.

Tess Whitehurst

May 1
Tuesday

3rd ♏︎

☽ → ♐︎ 11:20 am

Color of the day: Maroon
Incense of the day: Geranium

Beltane

Fire Mail to the Gods

Beltane is all about energy! Whether it's energy in love, energy in the ground and planted seeds, or energy in the balefire itself, energy is building and growing all around us at this time of year.

Harness the power of that energy by writing out a list of your requests to send on to the gods through fire. If you can't build a fire, use a self-igniting charcoal tablet in a cauldron. Write up your list, then toss some sacred herbs into the fire (or onto the tablet). Frankincense, myrrh, copal, or dragon's blood are all good choices. Allow the herbs to burn, and relish in their scent. Feel free to dance around or drum to build even more energy. Toss your list into the fire (or onto the tablet) and ask your deities to grant your wishes. End with a heartfelt and enthusiastic "so mote it be!"

Kerri Connor

May 2
Wednesday

3rd ♐︎

Color of the day: Brown
Incense of the day: Honeysuckle

Thank the Fire

Beltane is traditionally a fire festival. Many times we offer gifts to the fire of things we want to banish from our lives, but have you ever thought about thanking the fire for taking all of that baggage from you? The principle is the same. Write down what you appreciate about the fire, or make it an offering of gratitude to burn. Cast your circle (if you use one), light your ritual fire, and let the gratitude commence.

Once when we did this ritual, we fed sparklers to the fire. Great fun was had by all. And in subsequent fire rituals, every now and again a sparkler that hadn't burned during the first ritual would catch fire and blaze— a reminder that the element of fire does indeed have a memory.

Charlie Rainbow Wolf

May 3
Thursday

3rd ♐

☽ v/c 8:50 pm

☽ → ♑ 10:06 pm

Color of the day: White
Incense of the day: Nutmeg

Sun Day

Clearly, it's not Sunday. But in 1978, May 3rd was Sun Day, designated by President Jimmy Carter to raise awareness about and promote solar power. Those of us who honor the ancient ways are particularly attuned to the vast power of the sun to govern the cycles and seasons and to lend light and warmth to our spirits and lives. How appropriate, then, for modern technology to employ a few of the sun's life-giving rays toward lighting and warming our cities and homes. What's more, solar power can obviously support the earth and all her inhabitants by reducing our dependence on dirty energy and endless wars, and minimizing all the atrocities that follow in their wake.

Today, light a yellow candle to support a species-wide shift to solar and other clean energy sources. Also set the intention to shift your own setup to clean energy whenever financially and physically feasible.

Tess Whitehurst

May 4
Friday

3rd ♑

Color of the day: Purple
Incense of the day: Violet

Aligning our Resonance

One definition of the word *resonance* is "the state of a system in which an abnormally large vibration is produced in response to an external stimulus, occurring when the frequency of the stimulus is the same, or nearly the same, as the natural vibration frequency of the system." We can apply this concept toward greater alignment with our surroundings, connecting our inner power to the land. A charm can be created to tie our personal vibration to that of the land.

For this charm, obtain a stone or some soil from the desired area, placing it in a black-fabric pouch. Add personal items such as hair, saliva, or nail clippings. Hold the bundle, charging it and saying:

Magical hum of sacred land, my body responds to your frequency; this charm is charged by my hand to strengthen the bond of energy.

Bury the charm or hide it in your home.

Michael Furie

May 5
Saturday

3rd ♑

Color of the day: Black
Incense of the day: Pine

Cinco de Mayo

A Planting Spell

In many climates in the Northern Hemisphere, May is a great month to begin planting or making plans to do so. You don't have to be a master gardener by any means; it's quite easy to grow simple veggies such as tomatoes, leafy greens, carrots, radishes, mushrooms, peppers, and others—even if you're only using planters inside an apartment! Do some research online and begin your sustainable mission.

When you get your seeds or starts and have secured a place for them in your home or garden, close your eyes and lightly touch the leaves or topsoil. Feel the energy of the plant's spirit. Does it give you any messages? Is it telling you how best to care for it? In your mind's eye, do you see images of certain charms, gemstones, or decorative objects that the plant would like to have nestled in its soil?

When you feel ready, repeat these words:

Grow, survive, bloom, and thrive!

Repeat this frequently as you care daily for the vegetable and its spirit.

Raven Digitalis

 # May 6
Sunday

3rd ♑

☽ v/c 9:48 am

☽ → ♒ 10:48 am

Color of the day: Yellow
Incense of the day: Juniper

Spell for Self-Love

Ah, spring! We see beauty and rejuvenation all around us, and our bodies respond to the growth and warmth. It's a good time for a love spell. Witches know that the first rule of love spells is to use them on ourselves. We shouldn't interfere with anyone's free will, and we can't make someone else happy if we're unhappy with our own lives. This spell helps us take a self-inventory and work toward personal transformation.

Light a pink seven-day candle. Take a piece of paper and write down seven things about yourself that people find lovable. These may be physical attributes (your eyes, your hair) or personality traits (your generosity, your humor). Then turn the paper over and write seven qualities that need improving. Be honest; maybe you tend to be impatient or maybe you want to quit smoking. Place the paper on your altar, with the positive list facing up, and place the candle over it. The next day, turn the paper over and repeat, to remind yourself of your goals while the candle burns down.

Peg Aloi

May 7
Monday

3rd ♒

4th Quarter 10:09 pm

Color of the day: Ivory
Incense of the day: Neroli

Mirror Work

Monday, moon day, is a great day to work with illusion, emotions, and fertility and to do mirror work, as the silver of the mirror is like the shiny surface of the moon. Combine all of these into a mirror-based self-acceptance spell.

Look deeply into your own eyes, saying:

I see all that I am, have been, and can be.

I look at the creases beside my eyes. I live, learn, and grow from every experience.

Look at the lines around your mouth and say:

I laugh and smile, enjoying life.

Look at your lips and say:

I taste the deliciousness of a life well lived.

Look at your ears and say:

I hear the words of love, praise, and affirmation.

Look at the center of your forehead (where your third eye is) and say:

I honor my sacred spiritual path.

Now take your hands and cradle your face. Then say:

I am blessed as I am, worthy and wonderful. Me.

Dallas Jennifer Cobb

NOTES:

May 8
Tuesday

4th ♒

☽ v/c 10:29 pm

☽ → ♓ 11:11 pm

Color of the day: Gray
Incense of the day: Basil

Welcoming the Fae

Spring is a time to plant and cultivate. As you tend to your gardens, you may want to consider creating a space for the fae to occupy and thrive in. Consider spaces that are between your main property and the main garden. Plant roses, bluebells, peonies, and other flowers that attract faeries. Include shiny objects such as stones and gazing balls that will also attract them to your garden. Leave them offerings of milk and honey often so they know they are welcome, and they will return the favor by returning lost objects and helping to protect your property.

Charlynn Walls

May 9
Wednesday

4th ♓

Color of the day: Topaz
Incense of the day: Lavender

Love Resides here

Honeysuckle has to be my favorite climbing vine. I can't help but be under its spell, with its trumpeting blossoms and intoxicating scent.

A family was said to be lucky if they had honeysuckle growing over their door, as it kept sickness at bay. Honeysuckle is also associated with love, so here's a fun way to show that "love resides here."

To make an enchanted wreath for your front door, you will need:

• A grapevine wreath (abundance)

• Honeysuckle vines (love)

• Dried lavender flowers (peace)

• Dried rose buds (love)

Entwine the wreath with the honeysuckle vines, and glue the rose buds and lavender flowers on in a way that is pleasing to you. Now enchant your wreath by saying:

Across this threshold, love resides here.

Our hearts are entwined with love and good cheer.

With this charm, the magick
increases three times three.

This is a house of love, so mote it be!

Hang your enchanted wreath on
your front door.

Monica Crosson

NOTES:

 May 10

Thursday

4ℏ ♓

Color of the day: Green
Incense of the day: Jasmine

Cutting Ties Spell

Often we find ourselves held back
by relationships and situations
that have a negative impact on our
lives, unable to let go because of guilt
or a sense of obligation. Now, with
the waning moon in Pisces, it is good
to take stock, to communicate with
our higher Self, and to allow ourselves
to let go of that which is no longer
needed.

In your sacred circle, with black
candles lit (black for our mysteries),
ponder these energies. When you're
ready, tie a black cord around your
chest. Then tie individual black cords
to small drawings or notes with word-
ing that reminds you of these unnecessary aspects of your life, and attach
them to the cord around your body.
Take your white-handled knife and
cut the ties, one at a time, saying:

> I release you with love, respect,
> and gratitude for lessons
> learned. So mote it be.

Thuri Calafia

May 11
Friday

4th ♓

☽ v/c 5:02 am

☽ → ♈ 8:40 am

Color of the day: Rose
Incense of the day: Yarrow

Get That Project Started

There are too many days when we're facing a project, either magical or mundane, but we just can't get focused. We need to get to work, but what can we do? Make an amulet.

Get out your favorite quartz crystal, one that you've successfully used before in spells and rituals. Go to your favorite bead shop and buy seven beautiful, smallish beads, one in each of the chakra colors (red, orange, yellow, green, blue, indigo, violet). Buy a spool of silver wire. Wrap the quartz crystal with the silver wire with the beads strung on it in intervals. Make a loop at the top through which you can pass a chain, so you can wear this amulet as a necklace.

Set Sarasvati on your altar and cast your circle. Charge your new amulet with the energy of generosity and put it on. Sit quietly and invite ideas to come. Have a pen and paper handy and let your mind wander. When a good idea appears, write it down.

Barbara Ardinger

May 12
Saturday

4th ♈

Color of the day: Blue
Incense of the day: Patchouli

Knot Worth It Spell

We've all encountered situations where it's best not to get involved or to which we should not devote any energy. But sometimes staying out of it is easier said than done. Use this simple spell to disentangle yourself from any avoidable trouble.

Take a length of black (protective) wool in your hands and think of your particular situation. Speak it aloud and tie one loose knot as you do so, seeing it entwined in the fibers. Repeat the process two more times. Slide your fingers over and through the knots; feel how constricting they are. Then untie each one, saying:

It's not worth it. I want no part of it.

When all of the knots are untied, hang the cord on a tree or bush to be claimed by nature through wind and wood.

Natalie Zaman

May 13

Sunday

4th ♈

☽ v/c 2:05 pm

☽ → ♉ 2:15 pm

Color of the day: Gold
Incense of the day: Frankincense

Mother's Day

Nurturing Life

Mother's Day is a fine time to remember women as life givers, whether literally or metaphorically.

Prepare a small space in your garden, or fill a large pot or planter with planting mix. Plant a few small seeds (flowers or veggies) and water gently. Imagine the seeds resting in the warm soil, coming to life, and beginning to spout. Check them daily until you see sprouts emerge—as the moon waxes, this effect will be even stronger. Water as needed, watching as the plants take on vigor and begin to grow.

To encourage the young plants, offer small bits of organic plant food, sprinkle with dried chamomile or thyme, or set small agates near them. Offer thanks:

Great Gaia, life giver, mother of all.

*As you grace the spark of life
in these young plants,*

Guide my nurturing.

*See that these plants grow
strong and vital.*

*And remind me of the
responsibilities involved*

In being a bringer of life.

Susan Pesznecker

NOTES:

May 14
Monday

♃ ♄ ☿

Color of the day: Lavender
Incense of the day: Clary sage

A Money Sachet for the Wallet

For many of us, a magickal boost in the financial region sure couldn't hurt! Whether you use a purse, wallet, bag, or something similar to carry your cash and cards, you can create a small sachet spell bag to increase financial flow and project the energy of abundance.

Find a drawstring bag that fits in your wallet or purse. Fill it with any combination of these prosperous herbs: bergamot, cinquefoil, flax, jade, bay leaf, and patchouli. Add a dollar bill to the sachet, as well as an American penny produced between 1962 and 1981. Pennies were composed primarily of copper (bronze) during this time, and copper is known to be a superconductor of both electrical and spiritual energy.

Enchant your sachet by dedicating it to the elements however you see fit. Perform visualizations to illuminate the bag with rich, dark forest-green energy, and leave the bag outside for four days and nights to absorb the energy of the sun and these surrounding days of the new moon.

Raven Digitalis

 May 15
Tuesday

♃ ♄ ☿

New Moon 7:48 am
☽ v/c 4:30 pm
☽ → ♊ 4:43 pm

Color of the day: White
Incense of the day: Bayberry

New Moon Cleansing Bath

The new moon is a lovely time for cleansings and new beginnings. This spell will set you up for both. There's no better way to start a new moon cycle than with an energetically fresh and clean slate! If you've been in a funk, think of this as a bit of a reset.

Make yourself a simple bath salt scrub by gathering a cup of sea salt, a couple tablespoons of lavender buds, and two to four drops of lavender oil. Combine and mix thoroughly, then put into a small jar. Empower and charge the mixture as you see fit on your altar. Now, use as a scrub or soak in the shower or bath, and envision all the muck of the recent past going down the drain. You can chant the following as you cleanse with the bath salts:

By salt I cleanse and clear,

With lavender I calm and refresh.

When the lunar cycle is new,

So may it be a new start for me too.

Blessed be.

Blake Octavian Blair

NOTES:

May 16
Wednesday

1st ♊

Color of the day: Yellow
Incense of the day: Marjoram

Ramadan begins

Fern Spell

Ferns have been used for centuries by magicians to remove evil spirits. If you feel you're dealing with any dark spirits, this ritual should help you cleanse a space. You'll need two or three fern fronds dried, and some dried white sage. Cast a circle. For protection, sprinkle the white sage around the circle. In your cauldron or a heat-proof dish, build a small fire. Now begin to crumble the fern into the fire. As you do so, in a strong voice say:

> *Spirits dark,*
>
> *I am feeding this fern to the fire's spark.*
>
> *And I wish you to hear,*
>
> *I stand before you without fear.*
>
> *Spirits dark,*
>
> *You are commanded to leave this place.*
>
> *By the power of the fern, I cleanse this space.*

Close the circle and let the ashes cool for seven days. Then throw the ashes into a river or stream. Walk away immediately.

James Kambos

May 17
Thursday

1st ♊

☽ v/c 2:18 pm

☽ → ♋ 5:47 pm

Color of the day: Rose
Incense of the day: Yarrow

Grow, Grow, Grow

This is a simple garden blessing that requires a pitcher of milk, a jar of honey, and a hand drum, tambourine, maraca, or other small percussion instrument.

Walk the perimeter of your garden while slowly pouring milk onto the ground, creating a boundary. As you walk, say:

*Blessed by mother's milk, my
garden will grow and flourish.*

(In this case, mother's milk refers to the concept of Earth Mother to cow to milk, not a breastfeeding mother.)

Again walk the perimeter of the garden while slowly pouring honey onto the ground, adding to the boundary. This time say:

*Blessed by father's nectar, my
garden will grow in abundance.*

The third time around, play your drum or other instrument and chant:

*Grow, grow, grow.
Let abundance flow.*

Move to the center of the garden, dig a small hole, pour the rest of the milk and honey into it, and cover it up. This garden blessing will help you sow fertility and abundance.

Kerri Connor

NOTES:

May 18
Friday

1st ♋

Color of the day: Coral
Incense of the day: Vanilla

Tea in the Garden

Once you've had your morning tea (or coffee), don't dispose of the dregs. They're very useful in the garden. Coffee grounds hold plenty of nutrients for acid-loving plants such as rhododendrons and blueberries. Add some grounds and tea leaves to your compost pile to encourage the worms to come and aerate it. Leaves from herbal tea as well as black tea can be used in the same manner.

Many herbal teas can double as plant food, too. Break open herbal tea bags after they've been used, and scatter the leaves around the base of plants to feed the soil. Chamomile tea is an excellent protector against fungus. Teas can also be made from substances that you wouldn't want to ingest, such as fish guts or rabbit poop! Unappetizing to you, yes, but your garden will thank you for it!

Charlie Rainbow Wolf

May 19
Saturday

1st ♋

☽ v/c 5:14 pm
☽ → ♌ 7:11 pm

Color of the day: Indigo
Incense of the day: Sage

home Sweet home

Today, bless your home with sweetness, comfort, and abundance. Place a pink pillar candle on a plate or large candleholder, place it on top of your stove (perhaps in the center of the range), and surround it in a ring of sugar. Then bake a batch of your favorite cookies. If the recipe doesn't already call for cinnamon and vanilla, make sure to add at least a dash of the spice and a drop of the extract.

As the cookies are baking, center yourself and visualize the scent and energy from the candle and baking cookies spreading throughout your home and attuning it to the frequencies of sweetness, comfort, and abundance. Say:

Spirits calm and spirits bright, bless this home through day and night. Bring us comfort true and sweet, as we enjoy this magic treat.

After the cookies cool, enjoy them with your household or invite friends over to share.

Tess Whitehurst

May 20
Sunday

1st ♌

☉ → ♊ 10:15 pm

☽ v/c 11:30 pm

Color of the day: Amber
Incense of the day: Almond

Shavuot

Magical Journal

Every magic user needs a journal. It's a great place to jot down ideas, describe spells, track divination, and more.

I strongly suggest you choose a hard-copy journal. Yes, computers are great, but we know that writing captured by hand is remembered better and also tends to generate more creative ideas and responses. Give it a try!

Create a front page for your journal, if you wish, perhaps listing your name and the text's purpose.

Cut a piece of string or ribbon, preferably black. Use the string to do a four-way tie around the journal, package-style, tying it shut so it cannot be opened idly. Fasten with a square knot and, if you wish, with a bow. This simple mechanical barrier will help protect the journal from snoopers.

Hold the journal close and repeat:

Bless my words in sacred space,
here within this treasured place.

Charge the journal on your altar for a day, then tuck it away in a secure location.

Susan Pesznecker

NOTES:

May 21
Monday

1st ♌

☽ → ♍ 10:03 pm

2nd Quarter 11:49 pm

Color of the day: Gray
Incense of the day: Rosemary

Make Your Garden Grow

One of the most beautiful songs Leonard Bernstein ever wrote was "Make Our Garden Grow." It's the finale of the 1956 operetta *Candide*, which is based on Voltaire's 1759 novel, in which the characters search for "the best of all possible worlds." What they finally learn is to seek a simpler life and plant a garden. These are good intentions for us, too.

Most plants have symbolic meanings. As you plant your garden, whether it's outside or in pots on your balcony or on a table under a window, consider what energy you're planting. Start with a prayer plant. Go online and read about the traditional meanings and uses of other plants and herbs. Add those that resonate with you. For example, try catnip for happiness.

Tend your garden regularly. Talk to the plants and ask them to help you deal with issues that arise. Ask them to lend you their magic. Trade magical plants with your friends and use the plants in rituals.

Barbara Ardinger

May 22
Tuesday

2nd ♍

Color of the day: Red
Incense of the day: Cedar

Connect to Your Patron God Spell

Whether we've worked with our patron god(s) before or not, now, while the solar energies of the year are still waxing, is a good time to connect and deepen our bond. We can do devotional rituals, using words of praise and expressions of love. If your patron is a sun god archetype, you'll want to use a gold candle, and if your patron is a dark god, you'll want to use a black one. Inscribe the candle with words or symbols describing his awesomeness, and meditate on those energies for a while. Think about your special connection with him, and what kinds of energy patterns you would like help with. When you're ready, light the candle, saying:

I light this candle to represent
the light in me that is like you.
Please, (patron god), help me
grow more like you every day.

Allow the candle to burn down completely, knowing that as it does so, you are drinking in that light. Be blessed.

Thuri Calafia

May 23

Wednesday

2nd ♍

☽ v/c 10:55 am

Color of the day: Topaz
Incense of the day: Bay laurel

Money Consciousness Magic

As our modern society becomes increasingly cashless, we're becoming a bit removed from our awareness of money. So much is paid for with debit and credit cards that actually handing over cash has taken a lesser role.

To reestablish your connection to the immediate impact that spending money has on your life, have a "cash-only day" where you use only paper money or coins. When you spend money, as you hand it over, set the intention that this money will return to you and grow. Try to be fully aware of what you buy and how much you spend. It makes the impact so much clearer. To add to the magical effect, you can dab the corners of the bills with cinnamon or basil oil to help ensure financial return.

Michael Furie

 May 24

Thursday

2nd ♍

☽ → ♎ 2:52 am

Color of the day: Turquoise
Incense of the day: Clove

Creating Abundance

When you're in need of an increase in abundance, you can call on Thor on a Thursday. A couple of the items associated with him are the oak and the acorn. These items are perfect for abundance work. For this spell, you will utilize both oak leaves and an acorn.

To begin, create sacred space or simply sit underneath a local oak tree. Focus on the area of your life in which you need abundance. It could be monetary or it might be in another area. When you have in your mind what you are working toward, hold the acorn and oak leaves in your hand. See in your mind's eye the acorn sprouting, taking root, and starting to shoot up through the earth. Just as the acorn has taken root, so too has your work for abundance.

Charlynn Walls

May 25
Friday

2nd ♎

☽ v/c 5:04 pm

Color of the day: Pink
Incense of the day: Cypress

Apple Blossom Blessings

The apple tree is prominent in Celtic lore and is a powerful symbol of love, abundance, and contentment. This spell is meant to open you to the blessings of life and the beauty of your surroundings.

For this spell you will need a branch of apple blossoms, which you can obtain from the woods or a local orchard at this time (or you may buy an artificial branch from a craft store if apple trees don't grow in your area).

Lay the branch on your altar and light three votive candles in front of it. The candle flames symbolize the Celtic symbolism of the number three, which is about completeness and unity. Looking at the branch of blossoms illuminated by the candles, meditate on all the positive things in your life: your health, your loved ones, your home, your work, your hobbies and talents. Visualize these blessings as the abundant blossoms on an apple tree, a symbol of life's potential renewing itself each spring.

Place the cut branch in a vase of water so you can enjoy the fragrant blossoms for a few days.

Peg Aloi

NOTES:

May 26
Saturday

2nd ♎

☽ → ♏ 9:39 am

Color of the day: Black
Incense of the day: Sandalwood

Open Your heart Spell

Have you ever felt cheated by love? Maybe it was a relationship that went awry or the betrayal of a close friend or family member. It's easy to close our eyes and hearts at times like these, but there is so much beauty being missed. This spell will help you open your heart and rediscover the beauty all around.

You will need these supplies:

• A tealight candle

• Rose oil

• Paper and pen

• A fireproof container

• A rose quartz

Anoint your tealight with the rose oil. Write down on paper what was hurtful to you—get it all out. Now use the anointed tealight to burn the paper. Let it burn out in the fireproof container—in effect, letting love reign over hate and fear.

Now pick up the rose quartz. Focus on its loving energy, and visualize your heart open and seeing the world in a new way. As you do this, repeat:

I am worthy.

When finished, let the tealight safely burn out on its own.

Monica Crosson

NOTES:

May 27
Sunday

2nd ♏

Color of the day: Orange
Incense of the day: Hyacinth

Lest We Forget

Many people in the United States will be visiting the graves of those they loved and lost this weekend. Red, white, and blue is a popular color scheme, but do you know what the colors really mean? Red is for passion (and blood), white is for purity, and blue is for loyalty. These are the colors on many flags, and for good reason!

The graves of fallen soldiers are often decorated with flowers. Every flower has a different meaning. Red poppies, blue irises, white roses, and carnations bring both color and depth to a memorial. Poppies are a symbol of consolation and restful sleep, irises symbolize valor and hope, roses represent undying love, and carnations of all colors are associated with affection and distinction. Flags and flowers both send a message of gratitude to the fallen and help to bring peace after the heartbreak of loss.

Charlie Rainbow Wolf

May 28
Monday

2nd ♏

☽ v/c 1:25 pm
☽ → ♐ 6:29 pm

Color of the day: Silver
Incense of the day: Hyssop

Memorial Day

Paradigm Shift

I grew up thinking I hated hockey because I was always forced to go to the rink. It was cold, loud, and boring there.

Many years later, I housed a sweet young man who played on a high-end local hockey team. He begged me to come and see him play. I went because I liked him. As I watched him play, and recognized the multiple, high-level neurological skills involved, I fell in love with hockey. I realized that if I could experience a complete paradigm shift like this with one thing that I held to be "true," then quite possibly it could happen for other things.

Today, open yourself to the possibility of opposites: yin and yang, hot and cold, true and not true. Ask your higher self if there's anything you need to see the other side of. And with this asking, allow for the possibility of a paradigm shift.

Dallas Jennifer Cobb

May 29
Tuesday

2nd ♐

Full Moon 10:20 am

Color of the day: Scarlet
Incense of the day: Cinnamon

A May Full Moon Love Spell

It's spring and love is in the air. This love spell uses pansies and almonds, two powerful love-attracting ingredients. Combine them with a May full moon and you have a powerful love spell. Follow the instructions in the following verse, and see if love comes to you.

On a May eve when the moon is round,

*Go to a quiet garden where
pansies can be found.*

*Think of love and pick
a small bouquet,*

*Set them by your bed where
your head will lay.*

*Secretly, beneath your pillow
place nine almonds,*

*Dream a prophetic dream
to see if love will come.*

Each morn for the next nine days,

*Consume one almond, let
love find its way.*

And when this spell is done,

*May the universe bring to
you that special one.*

James Kambos

May 30
Wednesday

3rd ♐

☽ v/c 2:26 am

Color of the day: White
Incense of the day: Honeysuckle

honest Abe's Problem-Solving Penny

The Lincoln Memorial was dedicated on this day in 1922. Since then, folks visit Honest Abe's marble doppelganger not only to commemorate the man, but to tell him their troubles in the hope of getting some divine inspiration. You may not be able to travel to Washington, DC, today, but everyone has access to a penny.

Hold your coin (perhaps significantly dated) and gaze at Lincoln, a man known for his honesty and dedication to freedom and for being a person who spoke with spirit(s). Visualize your issue and whisper it into the penny's energy-drawing copper. Carry the penny with you and look for signs, symbols, and serendipitous happenings that will reveal your answers. Once you get them, take the penny and bury it or toss it into running water.

Natalie Zaman

May 31
Thursday

3rd ♐

☽ → ♑ 5:27 am

Color of the day: Green
Incense of the day: Apricot

Flowers of May

Catholicism dedicates this day to honoring the Virgin Mary. A common observance includes bedecking statues of her with floral garlands. Celebrations can be much more elaborate, such as processions in the Philippines where schoolchildren scatter flower petals and sing and chant prayers to her.

Many Pagans view Mary as simply another manifestation of the Goddess. To celebrate Flores de Mayo, or the "flowers of May," garland a Goddess image of your own, in any of her forms (Mary or otherwise!). Perhaps provide her with some incense and offerings and give thanks to the Great Mother and offer her prayers. Be creative in your expression: sing, dance, drum, chant—however your spirit moves you. Just be sure on this day to offer her the requisite beautiful flowers! Remember, any day is a good day to honor the Great Mother, in any of her forms. Blessed be.

Blake Octavian Blair

June

The month of June is a time that inspires warmth, love, passion, and deep appreciation of beauty. Agricultural festivals in old Europe acknowledge and celebrate the many flowers and fruits that become abundant at this time. It is no coincidence that these plants—such as roses, raspberries, strawberries, wildflowers, and those that feature red or pink flowers or fruit—are associated with the planet Venus and the goddess Aphrodite. June is also the traditional month for weddings, and the term *honeymoon* refers to the beverage mead, made from fermented honey, that was traditionally given to the bride and groom as an aphrodisiac.

June brings the start of summer, and for thousands of years the summer solstice has been a prominent festival in many cultures. This celestial festival signifies the beginning of warm weather and abundant growth yet also reminds us of its opposite calendar festival: the winter solstice. All hail the Holly King! Spells done in June are often connected to love, romance, growth, health, and abundance.

Peg Aloi

June 1
Friday

3rd ⅛

☽ v/c 11:37 pm

Color of the day: Rose
Incense of the day: Thyme

A Morning Scrying Spell

June mornings are like pearls: they're lustrous, almost ethereal. The mist from the night before lingers over ponds and rivers, and the hills aren't completely visible yet. Slowly the mist lifts like a curtain rising to start a new day.

A June morning is a good time to scry outdoors using water. To do this, find a body of water. It could be a pond, river, or birdbath. First, toss a pebble into the water. Let the ripples represent time itself, always moving. When ready, begin to scry. Think of a specific question, or be open to all images you see. When done, return to an everyday state of awareness and begin your day. Now you'll be more aware of your surroundings—the morning birdsong, the breeze on your skin, and the creation of a new day.

James Kambos

June 2
Saturday

3rd ⅛

☽ → ♒ 6:06 pm

Color of the day: Gray
Incense of the day: Ivy

Magic Radio

On this day back in 1896, Guglielmo Marconi applied for a patent for his invention, the radio. Now, when most people think of divination (telling the future), they think of tarot cards and ouija boards and other magical tools. Did you know that you can actually use ordinary things, such as your radio, to bring you messages from other realms?

Perhaps you've lost a loved one, and it seems that every time you think of this person, their favorite song comes on the radio. That's not a coincidence! Try using your radio when seeking answers to things as they're unfolding. Simply form the question in your mind, turn on your radio, and let the next song played provide your answer. You might be very surprised at the appropriateness of the results!

Charlie Rainbow Wolf

June 3
Sunday

3rd ≈

Color of the day: Yellow
Incense of the day: Heliotrope

Good Fortune

It's important to see our prosperity both in real life and in our minds. Go online and copy or print the Chinese symbol for prosperity and happiness on a piece of green paper and tuck it in your checkbook. Go to a craft store and find stickers of money and things that mean prosperity to you. Stick them on your computer, on your mirrors, and anyplace else where you will see them easily and often.

Go to the bank and get a silver dollar (preferably from the year of your birth), a silver Susan B. Anthony dollar, or a gold Sacagawea dollar—or all three. Carry at least one of these in your wallet—don't spend it!—or in your pocket. If you can get more than one of each, set them on your altar.

As you go about your days, be conscious of your prosperity, and don't waste your money!

Barbara Ardinger

June 4
Monday

3rd ≈

☽ v/c 1:10 am

Color of the day: Lavender
Incense of the day: Lily

Bonding with a Divinatory Tool

In order for a divinatory tool (tarot, pendulum, ogham, or others) to work effectively, it must work with you. This means that you and the tool must get to know each other. You must spend time together, bonding.

Begin by cleansing your new tool. A four-element cleanse works well: sprinkle the tool with charged saltwater (earth and water) and pass it through the smoke from a candle (air and fire). Be sure to cleanse yourself, too.

Once the tool is cleansed, hold it close to you, repeating:

Working together, each in turn,

Future paths may we discern.

For the next week, keep the tool with you at all times. At night, sleep with the tool next to you or under your pillow. Once the week ends, find a sheltered place for it in your sanctum.

Susan Pesznecker

June 5
Tuesday

3rd ♒

☽ → ♓ 6:53 am

Color of the day: Red
Incense of the day: Ginger

Elemental Balance Bag

Many earth-centered traditions recognize five elements: earth, air, fire, water, and spirit. On this fifth day of the month, let's take the opportunity to harness the energy of the number five in the form of these elements of natural magick. We can find more peace and walk smoothly through the world when we maintain an internal balance of these elemental energies.

You'll need a small pouch or medicine bag. If you do not have one, you can create one by laying your ingredients on a square of fabric, then drawing together the corners and tying them shut. For this elemental spell bag, gather representations of the five elements that resonate with you and lay them beside your bag or on top of your square of fabric. Recite the following, then pack and carry your bag:

Earth, air, fire, water, spirit.

Elements five, I ask you, please arrive.

*With your powers balanced,
I may thrive.*

Blessed be. So mote it be.

Blake Octavian Blair

 June 6
Wednesday

3rd ♓

4th Quarter 2:32 pm

Color of the day: Topaz
Incense of the day: Lavender

Receptive Communication

Communicating our needs can sometimes be difficult. Many times we do not want to burden others with our needs, as they can seem selfish. However, by connecting with the energies associated with Mercury and Wednesdays, we can better assert our needs.

When you wish to discuss something important regarding your feelings and needs, wear blue and silver clothing. Think about what you want to get across about your needs, whether you will be discussing a relationship issue or asking your boss for a raise. Right before you talk with the person, say:

I have no need to shout. This individual will hear me out.

The person you will be speaking to will be more receptive to hearing what you are trying to convey to them.

Charlynn Walls

June 7
Thursday

4th ♓

☽ v/c 2:35 am

☽ → ♈ 5:26 pm

Color of the day: Crimson
Incense of the day: Balsam

Travel Talisman

Summer vacations are starting, so make this easy talisman to help keep you safe throughout your travels. You will need the following:

- 1 small piece of black material
- 1 moonstone
- 1 small chunk of cedar wood
- 3 cloves
- 1 teaspoon of comfrey
- 2 drops of both clove and cedar oils (optional)
- 1 thin piece of black ribbon

Set your intention to keep yourself and your fellow travelers safe. Lay the material out flat and place the stone, wood, and cloves in the center of it. Sprinkle the comfrey on top of them. If you want to make your talisman even more powerful, add 2 drops of both clove and cedar oils on top of the comfrey, and allow the comfrey to soak it in. Fold the material in half and bunch up all the edges. Tie the ribbon in place to hold it shut. Carry the talisman on you while you are traveling.

Kerri Connor

June 8
Friday

4th ♈

Color of the day: Purple
Incense of the day: Rose

Smartphone Wallpaper Magic

Since for so many of us our cellphones are practically an appendage, we may as well use them as an extension of our magic. Given the amount of time we spend looking at our phones, they become a great tool for magical focus. A carefully chosen picture that is symbolic of a goal can be used as the home-screen wallpaper and charged with energy to help achieve it. This magic is then reinforced each time we look at the phone.

Once you find an appropriate picture and set it as the wallpaper on your phone, envision that this design is empowered with your magical goal and say:

Image of my intention, shining bright, release your power each time you light; whenever I glance upon this phone, the magic manifests, making the goal my own.

The spell will remain intact as long as the picture is set as the wallpaper.

Michael Furie

June 9
Saturday

4th ♈

☽ v/c 3:37 pm

Color of the day: Blue
Incense of the day: Rue

Peace Spell

Today is the birthday of my previous partner, whom I chose to leave because there was more bad than good. It's been many years since we separated, but I think of him every June 9th, and I choose to remember the good stuff. The law of attraction says "good attracts good" and "what we focus on grows."

So today, call to mind someone you used to be close to, someone you loved and who loved you, someone who is no longer part of your life. It could be a friend, coworker, family member, neighbor, lover, or spouse. Think about all the goodness they brought to your life. Remember their jokes, their favorite foods, and their birthday. Celebrate them. Appreciate what they taught you and brought you. Surround your mental image of them with the glowing white light of love and compassion. Bless them and release them. Your relationship is complete.

Dallas Jennifer Cobb

June 10
Sunday

4th ♈

☽ → ♉ 12:04 am

Color of the day: Orange
Incense of the day: Marigold

Banishing a Negative Body Image

Now, as we head into bikini season, picnic season, festival season, we often experience what feels like "judgment season" if we do not measure down to our culture's very narrow view of beauty. Today's Crone's Sickle moon in Taurus, a sign of sensuousness and health, can provide great power to dispel our negative body image attitudes.

First, take some time to think about all the people you love and how different their bodies are. Allow that love to flow to yourself, along with any anger or pain you feel over our culture's judgments. Light a black candle and chant:

Judgment and shame, begone dark blame—you cannot stick to me. I'm healthy and strong and I belong—by my will, so mote it be!

Continue chanting as the candle burns down and you begin to feel empowered. Blessed be.

Thuri Calafia

June 11
Monday

4th ♉

☽ v/c 11:29 pm

Color of the day: White
Incense of the day: Narcissus

Saint Barnabas's Fire Bundle

B ack when we still kept track of the
days with the Julian calendar, June
11 was the summer solstice and also
the start of the hay-making season,
both presided over by peacemaker
Saint Barnabas. Make a fire bundle
with some straw and the other traditional plants carried by folks on Saint
Barnabas's day: rose (love), lavender
(peace), and woodruff (protection
and plenty). Tie the herbs in a bundle
with a red cord. Let them dry out,
then burn them in a bonfire or your
cauldron to ensure a pleasant summer
blessed with abundance and sunshine.
As you set the bundle alight, invoke
Saint Barnabas's support with an
incantation based on a traditional song:

Barnabas bright, Barnabas bright,

The longest day and the shortest night.

*I'll make my hay while
the sun doth shine,*

*And the bounty of summer
shall truly be mine!*

Natalie Zaman

NOTES:

June 12
Tuesday

4th ♉

☽ → ♊ 2:53 am

Color of the day: Scarlet
Incense of the day: Ylang-ylang

Increasing Harmony in All Relationships

Human communication is complex. While mystical folks understand the reality of oneness, paradoxically everyone has their own unique personality and modes of communication. Life is built upon relationships—not just romantic ones but also familial bonds, friendships, acquaintances, pets, daily interactions with strangers, online exchanges, and so on.

To increase ease and grace in all manner of communication, procure eight orange-colored chime candles (the small birthday candles) and anoint them with an essential oil of your choice. Use whichever oil feels right to you, even if it's plain old olive oil! Beneath the candleholder, place cinnamon, catnip, and/or valerian (make sure the flames won't actually touch the herbs).

Safely burn one candle a day as you go about your communicative business at home. If you are not socializing in person or technologically, try singing, chanting, or reading out loud while the candle burns. Express yourself. Smell the herbs and feel the candle's subtle heat. Repeatedly declare:

My relationships are graced! I am
at ease through time and space.

Raven Digitalis

NOTES:

June 13
Wednesday

4th ♊

☽ v/c 3:43 pm

New Moon 3:43 pm

Color of the day: Yellow
Incense of the day: Lilac

New Moon Fasting Spell

Fasting on the new moon is believed to be very beneficial because the body's powers of detoxification are at their most powerful. Our physical vitality is very apparent at both new and full moons, so both days are perfect for paying close attention to how we treat our bodies.

On this day, eat lightly and consume only nourishing foods. Fresh fruit and vegetable juices, whole fruits, or raw salads are ideal, with maybe a few raw nuts for protein. Drink plenty of water.

When evening falls, look at the stars, made brighter by the moon's absence, and picture them illuminating your whole being from afar. Picture yourself glowing with health. Put some fresh fruit juice in a goblet, lift it to the sky, and drink, saying:

I drink to my health. I drink in the new moon's energy. I allow this energy to strengthen my will. I allow my body to release what I do not need.

Do this spell as a reminder on each new moon.

Peg Aloi

 June 14
Thursday

1st ♊

☽ → ♋ 3:20 am

Color of the day: Green
Incense of the day: Mulberry

Flag Day – Ramadan ends

Hag Stone Protection Cord

Hag stones are stones that have a natural hole running through them created by water erosion. They can be found on ocean beaches and in river or creek beds. Finding them can be difficult, so feel blessed if you happen upon one by accident—for those are the luckiest of all.

Thought of as a protective stone, hag stones were hung to protect against night terrors and Witches. When a hag stone was used as a seeing stone, it was said, one could look through the hole in the stone and see into the faerie realm.

To make a hag stone protection cord, you will need three feet of black cord and a hag stone.

Slip the cording through the hag stone and tie the cord off at the end. This will be your first knot. You will tie eight more knots, for a total of nine. As you tie each knot, focus on your intention.

When finished, hang your protection cord near your threshold.

Monica Crosson

 June 15
Friday

1st ♋

☽ v/c 12:18 pm

Color of the day: Coral
Incense of the day: Mint

Mermaid Love Altar

To draw a new romance or to get your love life flowing in the most ideal direction, make a mermaid altar today and petition your mermaid for the desires of your heart. Choose an image of a beautiful mermaid and place it on a flat surface over a pretty cloth. Add an apple or peach and a small offering of chocolate. Light a pink candle.

Close your eyes and center yourself in front of the altar. Then swim down to visit the mermaid in your mind's eye. Take a moment to honor her and to just enjoy being in her presence. When it feels right, speak from your heart and tell her what you'd like to experience in your love life. Then feel and sense her directing rushing water toward you. Feel it flowing around you and know that you are receiving a powerful attunement to the frequencies of that which you desire.

Tess Whitehurst

 June 16
Saturday

1st ♋

☽ → ♌ 3:21 am

Color of the day: Brown
Incense of the day: Magnolia

Don't Blame Me!

On this day in 1567, Mary, Queen of Scots, was imprisoned for supposedly plotting to murder Queen Elizabeth I of England. It's a difficult life when you feel you're entitled to something only to have it snatched out from under your nose. Have you ever been wrongly accused of something? There's a simple way to free yourself so that you're not imprisoned like Mary!

Using a red pen, write the name of your accuser backwards nine times on a piece of paper. Roll up the paper as tightly as it will go, then set fire to it in a heat-proof container. As the paper burns, so will your perceived guilt. Dispose of the ashes somewhere not on your property, like a public trash can, or even flush them down a gas station toilet. This spell works only if you're innocent, though, so think twice before doing it!

Charlie Rainbow Wolf

June 17
Sunday

1st ♌

☽ v/c 11:26 pm

Color of the day: Gold
Incense of the day: Eucalyptus

Father's Day

honoring Divine Guidance on Father's Day

Today is Father's Day in the United States. For many people, it is a joyous celebration of either their father or their own fatherhood. However, for many who have a strained or nonexistent relationship with their father, it can be a rather difficult reminder.

Our divine connections are always available, and we can honor the guidance we receive from those sources on this day. This is an excellent day to honor a deity or spirit who has given you the type of guidance, assistance, and reassurance fitting of a father figure. If you have not already done so, create a small altar to the divine entity and make a few simple offerings. Something of your own creation is an excellent choice. The more personal it is, the better. A craft, a food you've made, or an offering of poetry or song performed by you are all top-notch choices. Remember, you are supported!

Blake Octavian Blair

June 18
Monday

1st ♌

☽ → ♍ 4:41 am

Color of the day: Silver
Incense of the day: Clary sage

hand of Midas Success Spell

The Hand of Midas is a mythical artifact based on the hand of King Midas. According to Greek mythology, anything Midas touched instantly turned to gold. (This obviously created some logistical problems.) You can put the Hand to a more practical purpose for spells relating to success and abundance.

Trace your hand on a piece of metallic gold paper. Cut it out and place it on your altar, repeating:

As King Midas turned all to gold,

Power of success may this hand hold.

You may use the Hand in two ways.

One: write a request for success or abundance on a small piece of paper. Tie it scroll-style and set it on the Hand of Midas, repeating:

Hand of Midas, ever blessed,

May this charm find quick success.

Leave the scroll in place until the request is realized.

Two: use the Hand to "charge" magical items, charms, candles, and the like.

Susan Pesznecker

June 19
Tuesday

1st ♏

Color of the day: Gray
Incense of the day: Basil

Stop That Troll!

It's highly annoying to be pestered by trollish comments of wannabe "friends" on your Facebook page. The first thing to do is to delete every such comment and mark them as spam. If you own amber jewelry, wear it when you go online. Also keep at least one holey stone or piece of petrified wood nearby for added protection.

Now take stronger action. With Kali, Thor, and Nike on your altar, cast your circle and begin to visualize a tall oaken fence around your computer, tablet, or phone. Visualize aloe and other protective herbs growing along the fence. Hang agates on it.

Next, visualize divine action. Watch Kali eat parts of the troll and/or chase him away. Watch Thor cast thunder and lighting at him to paralyze him. Finally, invite Nike to stand beside you whenever you go online.

You can adapt this spell for use with all other social media.

Barbara Ardinger

June 20
Wednesday

1st ♏
☽ v/c 6:51 am
2nd Quarter 6:51 am
☽ → ♎ 8:29 am

Color of the day: White
Incense of the day: Bay laurel

Building a Victorian Flower Altar

Today in 1837, Queen Victoria ascended the throne. During that era, all objects carried meaning and every variety of flower conveyed a message. Build a Victorian love altar for platonic, romantic, or familial love by placing a photo of you and yours at the center and surrounding it with the appropriate flowers in the shape of a heart:

Tulips invoke the courage to declare your love.

Celebrate fidelity with ivy.

The first blush of love isn't pink, but purple and is hidden in the scent of lilacs.

Today, poppies are associated with the military, but before the First World War, patriotic love or love for someone in service was expressed by the nasturtium.

Daisies are an expression of innocent love. Surround images of the children you love with these flowers.

Affection begins with you. Show yourself some love with a narcissus.

And don't forget roses—love's essential, all-purpose flower!

Natalie Zaman

NOTES:

June 21
Thursday

2nd ♎

☉ → ♋ 6:07 am

☽ v/c 9:34 pm

Color of the day: Turquoise
Incense of the day: Myrrh

Litha – Summer Solstice

A Simple Litha Wish Spell

The practice of floating a wish to the Goddess in the form of a rose on a body of flowing water is a time-honored tradition and a nice way to celebrate the summer solstice in a simple yet powerful rite. To do this, choose a place in nature that has meaning and beauty for you. Take a rose for each wish you would like to manifest (other flowers are fine, too, if roses are not affordable or available) and cast a simple circle at the edge of a lake, stream, river, or ocean. Hold each rose while visualizing your wish successfully and beautifully manifested. As you release the wish to the water, say:

Now begins the season of fire.

May I be blessed with my desire.

Be sure to float one flower to the Goddess with no wish attached, to say thank you for her blessings.

Thuri Calafia

June 22
Friday

2nd ♎

☽ → ♏ 3:11 pm

Color of the day: Rose
Incense of the day: Alder

A Grass Spell for Protection

In this spell, grasses are used to share their strength and ability to protect home and family. On a dry day, cut some tall grasses to fit in a jar or vase. These could be roadside weeds or ornamental grass. Place the grasses in your jar or vase, but don't add water; you want them to dry. Hide the grasses—an attic would be ideal. Write the following charm and place it in the jar too:

Grasses green and grasses grand,

Growing tall and noble in
fields across the land,

I ask that you share your vitality

With those who share
this home with me.

Protect all who call this
home a place to dwell,

Through the year, keep us
safe and keep us well.

Next summer, compost the dried grasses and the written charm. Repeat the spell if you wish.

James Kambos

 # June 23
Saturday

2nd ♏

Color of the day: Indigo
Incense of the day: Sage

Pyromancy

Divination is a powerful tool, and by tapping into the energies associated with Hecate through the use of pyromancy, you can increase the power at your disposal. Pyromancy is the art of divination through the use of fire. To give your pyromancy a boost, you can connect with Hecate, who is associated with Saturdays and was often seen bearing a torch to light the path.

Create a sacred space that is free of distractions, and turn down the lights. Place a candle on your altar and light it. Concentrate on a question you have. Try to focus on what the flame is doing. Is it straight and unwavering, or does it flicker and pop? If it remains straight, with little flickering, you have a positive response to your question. If it flickers and pops, you may want to reevaluate the situation surrounding the question.

Charlynn Walls

June 24
Sunday

2nd ♏

☽ v/c 10:00 am

Color of the day: Yellow
Incense of the day: Frankincense

Ultimate Grounding Experience

This spell will help ground you and give you a good, strong connection to Mother Earth. If you don't own your own property that you can dig on, you will need an aluminum roasting pan or something of a similar size and shape, along with a bag of potting soil. Outside, fill the pan with soil and add water, stirring well until it's a gooey consistency. If you can dig into the earth, do so and add water until you have the same consistency.

Submerge at least your feet into the mud. If you can dig an actual mud pit, that's even better! Feel the mud squish between your toes. Meditate on what you are doing. Think about the ways our ancestors used mud. We tend to shy away from mud these days, but for many people it was an integral part of their culture. Rub it on your legs, arms, and face. Feel the connection with Mother Earth. Allow yourself to feel a part of Mother Earth.

Kerri Connor

June 25
Monday

2nd ♏

☽ → ♐ 12:29 am

Color of the day: Gray
Incense of the day: Hyssop

Honeybee Magic

Colony collapse disorder is causing an alarming loss of honeybee populations. We depend on honeybees to pollinate food-bearing plants, especially fruit trees. Bees have been important to humans for millennia and are intimately entwined with human history. Honey is a superfood and a natural antimicrobial agent. We can attract honeybees to pollinate in our gardens and encourage the healthy proliferation of these important insects.

Plant a variety of annuals in pots or in a small garden bed, and place a small bowl of water or a birdbath there, too. Annuals that attract bees include borage, sunflowers, cosmos, cornflowers, calendula, and asters. Some of these can be planted from seed earlier in spring, and many are available from your local garden shop.

Honeybees are gentle and will not sting unless their lives are in danger (as stinging kills them). Sit in your garden and watch them busily pollinate your flowers. Maybe they'll inspire you to be more industrious!

Peg Aloi

June 26
Tuesday

2nd ♐

☽ v/c 8:53 am

Color of the day: Maroon
Incense of the day: Geranium

Me Day

Today is my birthday, and I am celebrating. Join me.

Too often we do a lot for others. We give, work, do, help, and take care of and for others. But not today. Today is "me day," a chance to celebrate "self."

Quickly list the tiny, simple, and common things that bring you pleasure. Here are some of mine: delicious coffee, sunshine on my face, a fast walk that works up a little sweat, a swim in the lake, fresh chocolate croissants, belly laughs, time with friends, hugs, snuggles with my daughter, time in the garden with the cat, checking things off my to-do list, napping, and eating dinner on the deck.

Today, do as many of those small, simple, and sweet pleasures as possible, those tiny treasures that cost little and bring gratification to the soul. Store the kernels of joy away, and know that many small pleasures add up to BIG magic.

Dallas Jennifer Cobb

 June 27
Wednesday

2nd ♐

☽ → ♑ 11:52 am

Color of the day: Brown
Incense of the day: Honeysuckle

A Recycling Blessing Spell

Let's be honest: people who are spiritual, magickal, and earth-based should recycle everything they're able to. Even non-spiritual people with an ethical approach to life embrace recycling because it's the right thing to do. Try incorporating this blessing spell into your recycling activities.

The number thirteen is commonly used in Witchcraft because of its lunar associations. Gather thirteen items from your recycling bin. These may include things made of plastic, tin, aluminum, paper, glass, or other materials.

Think about the process of recycling. When these items become transformed into new items, how can you lend a bit of energy to the process? How can you send blessings to the people who will use (and ideally re-recycle) the transformed items?

Using a black permanent marker, write symbols and words of blessings on the items before putting them back into the bin. Empower them with energy and envision the magick rippling out into the world.

Raven Digitalis

June 28
Thursday

2nd ♑

☽ Full Moon 12:53 am

Color of the day: Purple
Incense of the day: Carnation

Magical Moon Bubbles

This spell is used to shift the body and mind to match the vibration of the moon, helping enhance our connection to the full moon and to the Goddess. First, create a brew using these ingredients:

- 1 sliced lemon
- 1 sliced cucumber
- 1 tablespoon coconut flakes
- 1 teaspoon poppy seeds

Put in a pot with three cups of water. Simmer on the stove until it begins to boil. Allow to cool, then strain into a large cup. Run a bath and pour the brew into the tub. Add some bubble bath and step into the water. Relax, mentally focusing on the moon. Visualize moonlight shining down upon you, enveloping you in its energy. When you feel connected, say:

Shining orb of power and might,
connecting me to the spiritual source,
bathe me in your sacred light, enchant
me with your magical force.

Drain the tub, dress, and go outside to gaze at the moon.

Michael Furie

 # June 29
Friday

3rd ♑

☽ v/c 4:58 am

Color of the day: Pink
Incense of the day: Yarrow

Faerie Garden Blessing

The beauty of summer is on full display! The roses are in bloom and crops such as lettuce, peas, and strawberries are table-ready. Why not invite the fae into your garden to give it a burst of magickal energy?

For this spell you will need:

- A flat stone
- Some pretty tumbled stones
- A little milk and honey
- A green tealight candle

Set your flat stone in a pretty place in your garden, maybe tucked under a fern or near some violets. Lay out the stones and the milk and honey. Light your tealight and say:

Greetings, faeries, far and near.

An offering I leave, my intentions clear.

Please bless this garden
with your faerie play,

And enchant our lives
each and every day.

Let the tealight burn out safely. Don't be surprised if you hear the faint sound of faerie bells as the sun begins to set.

Monica Crosson

June 30
Saturday

3rd ♑

☽ → ♒ 12:37 am

Color of the day: Blue
Incense of the day: Patchouli

Asteroid Day

A small group of scientists recently named today Asteroid Day in order to promote awareness about preventing these careening minor planets from hitting and harming our world. Indeed, the threat posed to us by asteroids is not small. Of course, as magical practitioners, we can lend a hand on the spiritual and energetic side of things. To do so, relax and take some deep breaths. When you feel calm and centered, call on Archangel Metatron, the angel of the cosmos, the spheres, and sacred geometry. Request that he proactively fine-tune the dance of asteroids in such a way that they cause the least possible harm to our world, now and into the distant future, for the highest and truest good of all. And if you'd like to learn more about protecting the globe from asteroids, or to spread awareness about this day, visit asteroidday.org.

Tess Whitehurst

I n 46 BCE, when Julius Caesar decided to reform the Roman lunar calendar, the names of the months were numbers. He moved the first of the year back to January, and, being the egoist he was, he renamed the fifth month (the month of his birth) for himself: Iulius (Julius, today's July). He also gave it a thirty-first day. (Then he named the next month after his heir, Augustus.)

July (the month of my birth, too) is high summer. In many places, it's the hottest month of the year. It's the month in which everything blooms until the heat of the sun makes flowers—and people—wilt and nearly melt.

What do I remember from my childhood Julys? Rereading my favorite books. Dragging the big old washtub out on the side lawn, filling it with cold water, and splashing all afternoon. Helping my father tend his flowers—roses, columbines, tulips, and hydrangeas. Climbing to the very top of our neighbor's huge weeping willow tree. Chasing fireflies before bedtime and putting them in jars to glitter and wink throughout the night. Sleeping in the screen porch with all the windows open to catch every possible breeze. What are your favorite July memories?

Barbara Ardinger

July 1
Sunday

3rd ≈≈

☽ v/c 6:56 pm

Color of the day: Gold
Incense of the day: Almond

All Creatures of the World Meditation

On this day in 1975, endangered species were declared internationally protected. Species disappear every day, and millions have been lost. It can be overwhelming to contemplate our impact on the planet and its creatures.

This day is one to celebrate all of the world's creatures, the great and the small. Go into the woods or a meadow or park, and sit down to observe. Listen with your eyes closed. How many creatures can you hear? Then look around you and see how many diverse species there are: birds, rodents, insects. How many can you name? Notice if these creatures interact with you. Do the birds come closer? Do butterflies land on you? Do curious squirrels approach you wondering if you have food?

Find something wondrous in each creature you observe: their colorful wings or feathers, their sounds and songs, their graceful movements. Consider your relationship to these living beings you share space with.

Peg Aloi

 July 2
Monday

3rd ≈≈

☽ → ♓ 1:31 pm

Color of the day: White
Incense of the day: Rosemary

World UFO Day

It's World UFO Day! If you can, sit under the stars tonight. Otherwise, place an image of space on your altar, light a candle, and sit before it. Relax your mind, breathe deeply, and see a glowing circle of protective light around you. Then envision a pillar of light encompassing you and connecting you with the core of the earth. See this pillar of light also extend straight upward and out of the atmosphere to connect you with the cosmos. Knowing and sensing that you are safely anchored with silver cords to the core of the planet, allow your consciousness to ascend into outer space. Go on an astral journey to connect with extraterrestrial wisdom. Perhaps you will visit another planet or find yourself on board a spaceship. Be open to what occurs, see who shows up, and be ready to learn what your new friends have to teach you.

Tess Whitehurst

July 3
Tuesday

3rd ♓

Color of the day: Scarlet
Incense of the day: Bayberry

Out with the Old

During the cooler months, we often notice that the air in the house gets stagnant and needs an airing out, but in the hotter months, especially if the windows are closed and the air conditioning is running nonstop, we still get that stagnant, sometimes smelly air.

Use today to open the windows at least for a little while. If it's really hot where you are, try for a couple of hours in the early morning or the later evening to help keep the temperature down. Otherwise, fling the windows open and let the breeze cleanse and refresh your indoor air. Add a few drops of lemon oil to water in a spray bottle and give all of your screens a spritz. As you work on each window, say:

Out with the old, in with the new.

Take a deep breath of the fresh air as it comes in.

Kerri Connor

July 4
Wednesday

3rd ♓

☽ v/c 5:47 am

Color of the day: Yellow
Incense of the day: Marjoram

Independence Day

Liberty and Justice for All

For readers in the United States, Independence Day can be a fun and frivolous time of celebration to mark the anniversary of colonial independence from England in 1776. However, Native American nations suffered greatly from these colonial conquests—and continue to suffer even now, in many cases.

We can't erase the past. We are where we are, and we must move forward with compassion. Historical violence and bloodshed have left an energetic mark of terror in colonized America and elsewhere. Let's lend a little bit of healing to these imprints regardless of our own nationality.

Light a red candle, a white candle, a blue candle, and a brown candle to symbolize the earth and her indigenous peoples (the brown is not a reference to skin color, but to the fertile earth). Place a map of the US next to the candles (even if it's on your phone or computer). Use your hands to pull heat off all four candles, and direct the warmth all over the map while visualizing harmony and repeating this:

> *Peace must prevail. Let freedom ring. With liberty and justice for all! So mote it be.*

Raven Digitalis

NOTES:

July 5
Thursday

3rd ♓

☽ → ♈ 12:50 am

Color of the day: Green
Incense of the day: Nutmeg

Protection Against Malevolence

We all have times when someone is angry with us and does not wish us well. In extreme cases, you may be the recipient of an angry hex or curse. What to do?

First, remember that cold iron is one of the best materials for repelling negative magical energy. Hanging an old-fashioned horseshoe above the door (on the inside) will keep your threshold safe from intrusion. An old railroad spike will work, too.

Second, work a basic grounds warding. Circle your home and property three times, moving widdershins (counterclockwise). As you walk, repeat:

Wards are set, safe at home.

You may wish to smudge or scatter salt as you walk. For added protection, bury a small Witch bottle (e.g., a bottle of nails, rosemary, and bits of obsidian) near the front of the house.

Third, stop in front of your door and use salt to create a pentagram in the area of the doormat. Step over the pentagram as you enter your home (and don't forget to lock the door!).

Susan Pesznecker

July 6
Friday

3rd ♈

4th Quarter 3:51 am

Color of the day: Purple
Incense of the day: Orchid

The Goddess Smiles Upon You

Friday is Freya's and Venus's day, a time to invoke love, joy, and beauty. Here in North America, these summer days are long with light. Invoke a sense of timelessness. Allow the light to stretch time and enable you to feel rich and lush, beautiful and loving. Move slowly through the day, pausing to say:

Time stretches luxuriously. There is time for all goodness today.

Let the goodness find you. Create beauty in each of your interactions. Look into people's eyes when you talk with them, greet strangers you pass by on the street with a smile or nod, hold the door for people, pat friendly dogs, and admire babies. Feel the energetic charge of each small positive interaction build within you, growing wider and longer. Internalize the positivity, and feel your own beauty, bask in your joy, and know you are loved. Let Freya and Venus smile upon you.

Dallas Jennifer Cobb

July 7
Saturday

4th ♈

☽ v/c 3:09 am

☽ → ♉ 8:51 am

Color of the day: Gray

Incense of the day: Pine

Boost Your Self-Confidence with Yarrow

There are times in our lives when we need a little boost of self-confidence. Maybe you have been asked to give a speech or you have an interview coming up. Yarrow is an herb that has been used for courage since ancient times.

For this spell you will need:

- An inscribing tool (such as a nail, straight pin, needle, or small knife—anything sharp)

- A red or orange candle

- Bergamot oil

- A red or orange drawstring bag

- A tiger's-eye gem

- Dried yarrow

Use your inscribing tool to carve personal symbols of self-confidence into the candle. Anoint the candle with bergamot oil. Light the candle and focus on all of your wonderful qualities.

Take your bag, gem, and yarrow, and hold them over the candle flame one at a time. Hold each item high over the flame in a closed fist—you don't want to accidentally catch a dried herb on fire in your hand! As you do this, repeat words of power, such as *strong, confident, capable, worthy,* or *courageous.* Put the yarrow and tiger's eye into the pouch, and carry it with you for confidence. Snuff out the candle for later use.

Monica Crosson

NOTES:

July 8
Sunday

4℞ ☿

Color of the day: Amber
Incense of the day: Juniper

Bells for Liberty

On this date in 1776, the Liberty Bell rang out in Philadelphia and the first public reading of the Declaration of Independence took place. Although we celebrate our nation's independence from Britain, we must remember that not all people in our nation have their civil liberties and are free from oppression. Many groups still face civil rights battles.

Today, let us ring our own bells as a reminder of these ongoing battles, and let it serve as an energetic and symbolic call to engage however we can to support civil rights and liberties for all citizens! As you ring your bells, you can recite your own list of groups still fighting for equality. Follow it with this incantation:

Peace, freedom, liberty, equality,

May it come swiftly.

With clarity of vision for everyone,

Let freedom ring out, let it be won.

Let it ring, let it sing,

*With pure hearts, these
things we work to bring!*

Blake Octavian Blair

July 9
Monday

4th ♉

☽ v/c 12:09 pm

☽ → ♊ 12:58 pm

Color of the day: Ivory
Incense of the day: Neroli

Breaking the Cycle of Addiction

With the Crone's Sickle moon in Gemini today, communication and cutting ties are both highlighted, so it's a really good time to do some soul-searching if you're finding yourself fighting an addiction.

For this spell, take a black or dark-blue pillar candle and carve it with symbols or words describing your addiction and your emotions around it. Tie one end of a black cord around the candle, and the other end around your wrist. Ground and center yourself, and open to the messages of the divine. Explore in meditation all the reasons for this addiction and all the avenues and attachments to this substance, as well as how the addiction manifests. When you're ready, cut the thread, saying:

Addiction, begone! (Name of addiction), you have power over me no longer! So mote it be!

Follow up by finding support through a group, therapist, or friend—quitting addictions is much harder to do alone.

Make sure you rid your space of the substance, take heart, and be blessed. Repeat as needed.

Thuri Calafia

NOTES:

July 10
Tuesday

4th ♊

☽ v/c 4:00 pm

Color of the day: Red
Incense of the day: Cedar

Connecting to the Warrior Within

When we are feeling attacked, we need to connect with the warrior within. Tuesday is a great day to connect with Mars to imbue your magickal working with strength and courage. Charge a piece of jewelry or a stone to create an amulet you can wear on a daily basis. Create a sacred space in which you can work. Connect to the warrior spirit and say:

*I charge this piece so that
any attacks cease.*

Wear or carry the item daily, and connect to the intention when you feel attacked.

Charlynn Walls

July 11
Wednesday

4th ♊

☽ → ♋ 1:59 pm

Color of the day: Topaz
Incense of the day: Lilac

Thank the Electricity Fairies

We're lucky to have electrical power, whether it's run by natural resources or fairies. Say thank you to the elemental electrical powers by putting THANK YOU stickers on your appliances and devices. Go online or to your local craft store and buy several sheets of THANK YOU stickers in colors and designs you like.

Set Mercury on your altar and cast a circle around your home. Starting in the kitchen, attach a sticker to the fridge, the stove, the microwave, etc. Attach stickers to your lamps and clocks, to your computer, tablet, and phone, to your TV, radio, and DVD and CD players. As you attach each sticker, give thanks for electricity and batteries. You can also thank whoever gave you the appliance or device or the store where you bought it. Give thanks all the way around the circle and be grateful that everything works.

Barbara Ardinger

July 12
Thursday

4th ♋

☽ v/c 10:48 pm

🌑ew Moon 10:48 pm

Color of the day: White

Incense of the day: Jasmine

Solar Eclipse

New Moon Pre-Magic Bath

The new moon is a time to work magic for beginnings, and its best to do so with a cool, clear head. Make a bath sachet to cleanse yourself inside and out before you do any magical work.

Chop some cooling mint leaves, cleansing lavender, and brightening lemon balm, and mix them with a spoonful or two of coconut oil. (You should have more herbs than oil; the oil acts as a binder.) Place the mixture in the fridge to chill. When it solidifies, form it into a ball and knot it in a double layer of cheesecloth. Toss the sachet in your bath, then immerse yourself in the water and rub the sachet over your body with these words:

New beginnings, I am ready,
cool, cleansed, and brilliant!

Visualize the sachet cooling off any hot spots, healing any hurts, and washing away any and all distractions. Now you're ready for magic!

Natalie Zaman

July 13
Friday

1st ♋

☽ → ♌ 1:31 pm

Color of the day: Pink

Incense of the day: Vanilla

Make Me a Star

Today in 1923, the iconic Hollywood sign was erected in the hills of Los Angeles. You don't have to have a huge sign or be a builder to make an impact, though! You just need determination and motivation. Today's waxing moon in Leo is the perfect time to launch a new project that will get you notoriety and attention.

You'll need a candle and an old key, preferably one that never belonged to you (look in thrift shops or online; they're inexpensive enough). When the moon enters Leo today, light the candle and recite these words:

Fire sign and candlelight,

Hear my heartfelt words tonight.

Start my plan successfully,

Then make it known, so mote it be!

Pinch out the candle flame, and keep the key with you to remind you that you're now on the path to achievement and recognition!

Charlie Rainbow Wolf

July 14
Saturday

1st ♌

☽ v/c 7:12 pm

Color of the day: Black
Incense of the day: Sandalwood

Kitchen Witch's Protection Bottle

Here is an easy way to create some protection magic in your kitchen using only four ingredients:

- 1 cup unpopped popcorn
- 1 cup dried beans
- 1 cup dry rice
- 1 canning jar (quart size or larger)

Layer the popcorn, beans, and rice in the jar, then hold the container, enchanting it to become a powerful protective force. Focus on protective energy and say:

Guarded this land shall ever be, gifts from the earth; plants of strength and vitality, protect this home and hearth.

Seal the jar tightly and place it in full view in your kitchen or over a fireplace mantel to serve as a protective amulet.

Michael Furie

July 15
Sunday

1st ♌

☽ → ♍ 1:31 pm

Color of the day: Yellow
Incense of the day: Hyacinth

honor the Ancestors

In Eastern Japan, the Bon festival is celebrated right around this time. This is a time of honoring one's ancestors, recognizing their sacrifices for future generations, and facilitating their most ideal and harmonious presence in the afterlife.

If you can, visit one or more of your ancestors' graves today. Otherwise, place their pictures or heirlooms on your altar. Adorn the headstone or altar with one or more white roses, and light a white candle in their honor. Relax, center, and connect with the spirit of your ancestor (or each ancestor in turn). Imagine bright white light filling and surrounding their spirit, removing any heavy or stuck energy that you may perceive. Then see their spirit in its truest light: the light of pure wholeness and love. Laugh or dance with them and inwardly honor their path in life, seeing it as a perfect support and complement to your own life.

Tess Whitehurst

July 16
Monday

1st ♍

Color of the day: Gray
Incense of the day: Lily

A Thunderstorm Love Spell

U se this spell to add more passion and romance to your relationship. To charge this spell, it should be performed quickly as a thunderstorm approaches.

You'll need a piece of paper, a red ink pen/marker, some dried yarrow, and an envelope. As a thunderstorm moves close, draw a heart on the paper in red ink. Crumble the yarrow over the heart. Fold the paper, put it in the envelope, and lay it on a windowsill. Charge the spell with these words:

Thunderstorm, bring my love, excitement, and passion.

Hear my words and turn them into action.

Let the lightning flash, let the thunder roar.

Keep my love hot with desire, now and forever more.

As the storm moves away, hide the charm. After you see it's working, keep the spell active, if you wish, by replacing the yarrow once in a while.

James Kambos

July 17
Tuesday

1st ♍

☽ v/c 6:50 am

☽ → ♎ 3:42 pm

Color of the day: Maroon
Incense of the day: Ylang-ylang

Wash Away Anxiety Spell

N o matter who we are, anxiety can creep into our lives. Before we know it, those gnawing thoughts can turn into little demons that interrupt our sleep and make daily living feel intolerable.

Release unneeded anxiety with this easy spell. You will need:

- Stones (as many as you feel are necessary)

- A washable marker

- A large tub of water

Take as many stones as you need (garden pebbles work just fine), and with a washable marker write on each stone the anxieties you may have, such as nervousness about a new purchase or the first day of a new job or school.

Now take each stone and, one at a time, drop them into the water. Imagine yourself free of anxiety as the marker dissipates your fears in the tub of water. As you drop the last stone, say:

I release all fear and anxiety

In the name of the Goddess.

So mote it be.

Monica Crosson

Notes:

 ## July 18
Wednesday

1st ♎

Color of the day: Brown
Incense of the day: Lavender

Chart Your Course with the Tarot

The tarot can be a wonderful tool for looking ahead at paths yet to be walked and obstacles yet unmet (and unknown). To do this, you'll need your favorite tarot deck and work surface (silk cloth, etc.).

Prepare by considering what period of time you want to look at: The next several weeks? Months? An entire year? Set a time frame and spend a few moments contemplating. What do you imagine happening during that period? What questions do you have?

Spread out your card surface and shuffle and cut the deck as usual. Lay out one card for each time delimiter—e.g., one card for each week, month, season, etc. Contemplate the cards and consider initial meanings.

Make a detailed journal entry about which cards turned up for which times, and note your initial responses. You might also photograph the layout for later reference—the layout itself could hold meaning. Return to your notes and photos weekly to assess what the cards have revealed.

Susan Pesznecker

 July 19
Thursday

1st ♐ ♎

☽ v/c 3:52 pm
2nd Quarter 3:52 pm
☽ → ♏ 9:13 pm

Color of the day: Purple
Incense of the day: Clove

A Good Day Knot Spell

Sometimes it feels uncomfortable to be awake and go about the day. Other times it feels great to be alive and taking care of business! It is my sincere hope that you are feeling well and jovial on this fine summer day, but if you're not at your finest, please remember this simple knot spell for the next day you're feeling in tip-top shape.

On a day when you are feeling wonderful, get a cord, a rope, or a simple piece of string in which you can tie a loose knot. Let your positive energy well up inside you while you tie a simple knot. As you tie, make a strong effort to focus your positivity into the knot in order to "capture" the energy.

In the future, on a day when you feel crappy, untie the knot and breathe its energy into your mind and body for a self-induced magickal boost.

Raven Digitalis

July 20
Friday

2nd ♏

Color of the day: Rose
Incense of the day: Cypress

Spell to honor Aphrodite

This date is the old Greek Festival of Aphrodite, goddess of love, sex, and beauty. She was considered important for partnerships of all kinds because of her compassion.

To set up your altar for Aphrodite attunement, use the colors pink, pale green, and pale blue. Her gems include rhodocrosite, rhodonite, and rose quartz. Roses are her flower, especially pink or fragrant heirloom roses. Incense and oils should reflect flowers and fruits, all of which are sacred to Aphrodite and are under her astrological rulership (the planet Venus, which rules Libra and Taurus).

To invite Aphrodite's blessing, light a pink seven-day candle, visualize Aphrodite's loving sphere of peace, compassion, and love illuminating the room with a pale pink light. Softly chant her name (the traditional pronunciation for magic is "Ah-fro-DEE-tay") and become aware of the loving, peaceful energy invoked by thoughts of her.

Peg Aloi

July 21
Saturday

2nd ♏

Color of the day: Blue
Incense of the day: Rue

Magickal Entryway Wash

Saturdays are a lovely time to do magickal work for the hearth and home. Logically, the place that sees the most physical and energetic traffic is your front door. Today, give your front door a thorough cleansing with soap and water, then mix up a nice magickal wash to both cleanse and boost the energetic vibrations of your door's main gateway.

To call upon the magickal number of three and all that it represents, buy three different citrus fruits of your choosing, squeeze their juice into a bucket of hot water, then add their peels. Wipe down your door and entryway with the wash and recite this:

Citrus beaming with high energy,

Cleanse and clear my entry's energy.

By power of citrus three, so mote it be!

When you are finished, dispose of the bucket of wash under a tree in nature and let Mother Earth transmute any collected energy.

Blake Octavian Blair

July 22
Sunday

2nd ♏

☽ v/c 5:18 am

☽ → ♐ 6:12 am

☉ → ♌ 5:00 pm

Color of the day: Orange
Incense of the day: Marigold

Taming Technology

We don't want to bind or hex our devices, but some of us want to slow things down, so to speak, until we can get caught up with upgrades and apps and ... well, stuff. A spell to tame technology has to work in both directions: on our device and on us. Let's ask Sunday's ruler, the Sun, for help.

Set Saule or Apollo on your altar and cast your circle. Plants tend to grow slowly, so find plants that are ruled by the Sun (sunflowers, rosemary, a bromeliad) and set them on your altar. Add cashews and acorns and burn cinnamon or frankincense. Finally, set your device(s) at the feet of the deity and speak these words:

*Great and mighty powers
of technology,*

I am learning. I want to learn!

Please wait for me to catch up.

Lend me your artificial intelligence.

*Give me helpful menus and
remember my passwords.*

Barbara Ardinger

NOTES:

July 23
Monday

2nd ♐

Color of the day: Lavender
Incense of the day: Hyssop

Celebrating Neptune

During the heat of summer, we look for any way to cool down. We revel in the water and how it nurtures, calms, and cools us. Neptunalia was celebrated by the ancient Romans on this day, at the time of year when water was scarcest. By taking a moment to honor and invoke Neptune, you can garner his favor.

Create a sacred circle in which you can call upon Neptune. On your altar you may want to drape a blue cloth and include items such as shells and sand. When you feel ready, call upon Neptune and honor him. Be open to any messages that come from him. Feel free to offer him an item such as a blue stone as a token of your thanks.

Charlynn Walls

July 24
Tuesday

2nd ♐

☽ v/c 4:22 am
☽ → ♑ 5:49 pm

Color of the day: Gray
Incense of the day: Ginger

Cultivating Strength and Courage

Tuesday is ruled by Mars, the planet of strength and courage. Open both hands and look at your palms. In palmistry, the line encircling the base of the thumb is called the "line of Mars." With your left index finger, trace the line of Mars on your right hand. Traditionally the right hand "sends" energy. Draw to mind all that you do and give, the work you undertake, the help you provide, the meals you cook, and the chores you complete. You are valuable.

Now stroke the line of Mars on your left hand with your right index finger. Allow yourself to breathe. Inhale and receive the energy of others. Feel how they support, hold, and help you. Know that you are loved, admired, desired, respected, and enjoyed. Traditionally the left hand "receives" energy.

Press your palms together in the middle of your chest, giving and receiving energy. You are your deepest source of strength and courage.

Dallas Jennifer Cobb

July 25
Wednesday

2nd ♑

Color of the day: White
Incense of the day: Bay laurel

Prosperity Spell

The moon near full in Capricorn gives us lots of energy we can use for prosperity spells. For this work, choose some favorite money-drawing herbs in multiples of four. Patchouli, oats, allspice, and pine nuts are all good options, and adding a spell-sealing herb such as Echinacea will help set the magic and hold the energies together. Essential oils such as patchouli or sandalwood will give the mix an earthy fragrance.

Chant over the herbs as you mix them, with simple words such as these:

> By the grace of the divine,
> prosperity is mine.

Or chant more complex words of your choosing.

Once the herbs are fully imbued with your energy and intention, tie them up, along with a silver coin and a small crystal, in a square of green cloth with green, gold, or silver ribbon. Sprinkle some of the herbs or wear the charm anywhere you could possibly come into contact with money.

Thuri Calafia

July 26
Thursday

2nd ♑

☽ v/c 9:41 am

Color of the day: Crimson
Incense of the day: Apricot

Void-of-Course Moon

The moon is void of course (VoC) for a surprisingly long period today—from 9:41 a.m. EDT today to 6:41 a.m. tomorrow. VoC moons aren't that rare, but for those who are strongly influenced by the moon, there are some things you might want to avoid. VoC moons are never a good time to start projects or to try to push forward with ideas. You'll only end up frustrating yourself.

All is not lost, though. This is a wonderful time for meditation, intro-spection, reflection, and just slowing down. The VoC moon can also trig-ger karmic events, so make sure you act with integrity in order to avoid future repercussions. That's particu-larly important with this VoC moon, which occurs in Capricorn. Use this time for prioritizing what needs to be done, and you'll be rested and ready once the moon enters Aquarius and reaches its fullness tomorrow.

Charlie Rainbow Wolf

July 27
Friday

2nd ♑

☽ → ♒ 6:41 am

Full Moon 4:20 pm

Color of the day: Coral
Incense of the day: Rose

Lunar Eclipse

Shine Bright

The full moon is all about positive influences. The lunar eclipse, which won't be visible to most North Americans today due to the timing, is a sign that even though the moon is hidden in the shadows, she is still just as powerful. Therefore, the eclipse actually can give you a boost in any workings you do at this time. Make a special batch of magical water to use in future spells and rituals.

Fill a glass bottle with filtered water. Take it outside in the morning and raise it up over your head. Ask the Goddess to bless the water and infuse it with energy. Allow the bottle to sit out all day and all night. The water will be exposed to the sun, the moon, and the eclipse, harnessing the magical properties and strengths of all three. Before bringing the bottle in, thank the Goddess for charging this potent water.

Kerri Connor

July 28
Saturday

3rd ♒

Color of the day: Indigo
Incense of the day: Ivy

A Shell Spell

This spell will bring any wish into your life. You'll need nine seashells and your ritual cup filled with bottled spring water. Place the cup on your altar or a table and fill it with the spring water. Surround the cup with the shells to form a circle. Think of your wish, then ground and center. Hold your hands over the shells and cup, and say the following charm:

Shells, set in a circle so round,

To me, let my wish be bound.

Shells, totaling the sacred number nine,

Let my wish be mine.

Take a sip from the cup and set it back in place. Leave the shells and cup undisturbed for a day. The next day, place the shells with your ritual tools to use again. Use the water to water a plant. Return the cup to its usual place. The spell is now working in the unseen realm.

James Kambos

July 29
Sunday

3rd ♒

☽ v/c 5:25 am

☽ → ♓ 7:28 pm

Color of the day: Amber
Incense of the day: Heliotrope

Fellowship of the Ring

Today in 1954, J.R.R. Tolkien published *The Fellowship of the Ring*, wherein we learn that Bilbo Baggins's "precious" is a manipulative weapon, charged with the energy of the evil Sauron. Of course, there are other rings imbued with positive power, giving their wearers the strength they need to deal with the challenges they have to face. You can do the same.

Ask your fellowship—those whom you call your closest companions—to imbibe a token with their energies so you can carry them with you. Select a piece of jewelry that holds meaning for you (it does not have to be a ring). Have each friend hold the piece, breathe on it, and say:

To this token I give some grace,

Let it stand for (your name)
in my place.

Wear and feel the power of friendship. You can do this ritual as a group to multiply and share support.

Natalie Zaman

July 30
Monday

3rd ♓

Color of the day: Silver
Incense of the day: Narcissus

Cleansing with Sugar and Salt

To add a bit of cleansing magick to your daily routine, acquire a small jar of sea salt and a small jar of pure cane sugar. Get a vanilla bean and cut it in half. Bury half of the bean in the sugar and the other half in the salt. Enchant the salt by focusing energy with your right hand while drawing the energy from the cosmos above with your left hand. Focus your mind on the mighty healing powers of the earth element. While you do this, say:

Creature of salt, of sea, and of
earth, I empower you with purity
and protection. So mote it be!

Do the same with the sugar, but say:

Creature of sugar, of tropics, and
of earth, I empower you with
sweetness and grace. So mote it be!

Cap both jars. You may choose to add the sugar to food and drink so that you can invoke its gently cleansing vibrations. You may choose to sprinkle the salt at your doorways to allow only the good stuff inside your home. There are numerous possibilities, so follow your intuition and have fun!

Raven Digitalis

July 31
Tuesday

3rd ♓

☽ v/c 6:42 pm

Color of the day: Red
Incense of the day: Cinnamon

Thanking Your Plants

If you have a garden or even a single herb or vegetable plant, this is an appropriate time of the year to give gratitude not only to these specific plants but to their realm in general.

Fill a large cup or watering can with fresh water and place your hands over it, mentally sending white light into the vessel to charge the water with the power of blessing. Go to your garden and lightly water your plants, connecting with them and sensing the vital bond that humans share with their world. As you water the plants, say:

*Respect and due reverence shall
now be paid, my heartfelt thanks
for your sacrifice made; shoot and
leaf and full-grown stalk, sacred
plants who have served my needs;
harvest time shall now unlock, the
gifts from Earth their magic freed.*

Michael Furie

NOTES:

August

S ummer is at its height of power when August rolls in, bringing with it the first of the harvest festivals, Lughnasadh (or Lammas), on the first of the month. Lughnasadh is a festival of strength and abundance, a reflection of August itself. Lugh and the Corn God are highly celebrated during this month and are particularly good to work with in spells or rituals for abundance, prosperity, agriculture, marriage, or strength. The Earth Mother in her many forms is ripening and overflowing with abundance. While we often see the first harvest as being associated with corn, there is much more that has been harvested by this point. We must remember not to overlook anything or take anything for granted in our lives, and the harvest is an excellent reminder of that. It is a time to begin focusing on expressing appreciation and giving thanks for all that we have.

The full moon this month is most often called the Corn Moon, but also goes by the Wyrt Moon, Barley Moon, or Harvest Moon. The stones carnelian, fire agate, cat's eye, and jasper will add extra power to your spells and rituals at this time. Use the herbs chamomile, St. John's wort, bay, angelica, fennel, rue, barley, wheat, marigold, or sunflowers in your spells. The colors for August are yellow, gold, and the rich green of the grass and leaves.

Kerri Connor

August 1
Wednesday

3rd ♓

☽ → ♈ 6:54 am

Color of the day: Topaz
Incense of the day: Honeysuckle

Lammas

First harvest

Lammas is the traditional first harvest, when the early wheat was baked into loaves. Instead of harvesting wheat today, harvest what you've "grown" so far this year.

Set a tiny sheaf of wheat or other grain or something else that signifies harvest on your altar and cast your circle. Think about what's been happening in your life this year. Consult your journal or maybe old emails. What metaphorical seeds did you plant earlier this year? What has grown?

Shuffle your favorite tarot deck and draw one card for each month so far. If you like, draw major arcana cards for February, March, May, and June and minor arcana cards for January, April, and July. Lay them in a row and do a personal reading. Then draw one more card. This is a pointer to your potential future. What might come to you in the next two harvests this year?

Barbara Ardinger

August 2
Thursday

3rd ♈

☽ v/c 10:52 pm

Color of the day: Turquoise
Incense of the day: Myrrh

Water Balloon Blessings

You can easily add the element of water to any spell by using moon water or performing the spell in your bath tub, but this is a bit more fun for a hot summer day.

Gather your friends and/or family, along with an assortment of colored balloons and herbs. Using color and herb correspondence charts, choose a balloon color that goes along with your intention, as well as herbs to help back it up. Fill the balloon partway with water. Push in some herbs and then fill it the rest of the way. (It's easier to put the herbs in if the balloon is not filled all of the way.)

Partner up with someone (you can share your intention with them if you want, but you don't have to), and have them burst the water balloon on you and let the "blessing" wash over you. Then do the same for them!

Kerri Connor

August 3
Friday

3rd ♈

☽ → ♉ 3:51 pm

Color of the day: White
Incense of the day: Thyme

Fire Cleanse for Self-Love and Sexual Power

Today, the conditions are right to cleanse away old, unloving thoughts about your body, sexuality, and appearance. Kindle a bonfire or campfire, or make a fire in an outdoor fire pit. (Or just gather a lighter and a cauldron or pot that is safe for burning.) As you sit before the flames (or cauldron), make a list of every negative thing you regularly think about your body, sexuality, and/or appearance. Then say (or yell!):

I am now ready to let these things go!

With that, throw your list into the flames (or burn it in your pot). As it burns, feel the flames burning away all old negativity from your body and energy field and filling you with a passionate new love for yourself. Say:

I am a radiant divine child! I am divinely beautiful, lovable, and sexy! I now own my power and live my beauty! Blessed be.

Tess Whitehurst

August 4
Saturday

3rd ♉

4th Quarter 2:18 pm

Color of the day: Indigo
Incense of the day: Magnolia

Grounding with the Stone People

Saturdays are a good day for cleansing and protection magick. I consider grounding and centering oneself to be a form of this type of magick. One of my favorite ways to do this is to work with the spirits of the Stone People.

Take a hike in a natural area from which you'd be allowed to take a stone. When you find a stone that calls to you, ask it if it would like to work with you. If it agrees, this Stone Person will be your new helper for this spell. Leave an earth-friendly offering in its place.

Anoint the stone with holy water, then hold the stone and enter an altered state through meditation or rattling. Ask the stone to use its earthy powers to ground and center you, bringing you balance and protection by merging with its spirit. Keep the stone. Repeat as necessary.

Blake Octavian Blair

August 5
Sunday

4th ♉

☽ v/c 7:46 pm

☽ → ♊ 9:32 pm

Color of the day: Yellow

Incense of the day: Eucalyptus

Oyster Shrine for Creativity

English folklore tells us that eating oysters today will bring good luck for the rest of the year. Oysters have long symbolized luck and love, and in ancient Egypt oyster shells were worn as protective amulets. If you eat some oysters today, save and clean two shells to create a shrine grotto to the mother of pearl, the embodiment of creation.

Stand the shells up vertically (the widest part should be the base) and lean them together to make a conical grotto. Use a drop of glue to secure them. Place the grotto on your altar and set a tealight candle inside. Light the candle and say:

Maker of pearl,

The moon in a shell,

I create my fate

With your help and this spell!

Keep the shrine on your altar until the year's end, repeating the incantation each time you relight the candle or when you experience a burst of creativity.

August 6
Monday

4th ♊

Color of the day: Ivory

Incense of the day: Clary sage

The Reset Button

In the summer, I swim in Lake Ontario most days. I love submerging my crown chakra in the water and feeling the complete change in my energy. This seems to "reset" me, clearing my aura and raising my vibration. I've learned that a dip in the lake can restore me to sanity following an experience of hurt, anger, or disappointment.

We aren't computers, but it's good to know how to reset ourselves. What do you do when you are tired, angry, sad, or overwhelmed? What are the things that help you clear negativity and restore equilibrium? Make a list entitled "10 Things That Help Me Feel Better." Write down what works for you. Here is my list:

- Drink a cup of tea
- Shower
- Hug someone
- Swim
- Laugh
- Nap
- Journal
- Smudge

Natalie Zaman

- Meditate

- Eat chocolate

Post your list where you will see it regularly. Read it. Know it. Use it. And when you need to, press "Reset."

Dallas Jennifer Cobb

NOTES:

August 7
Tuesday

4th ♊
☽ v/c 3:54 am

Color of the day: White
Incense of the day: Basil

A Personal harvest Spell

The harvest season has begun, but not just an agricultural one. This is also a time for personal harvests. Have you attained your goals? Is there more you wish to do? This spell will help you achieve your dreams.

First, decorate your altar with seasonal produce and flowers. You'll also need three sheets of paper, a pen, and a self-addressed stamped envelope. On the first sheet, write a list of everything you're thankful for. On the second sheet, list all that you've achieved. On the last sheet, write a list of everything you still wish for, and how you'll achieve these goals. Fold this sheet like a letter, seal it in the envelope, and send it to yourself. This will be your "harvest" still to come. When it arrives, don't open it until Samhain, the last harvest. Then see how you did. Keep the three lists as long as you want, then discard them.

James Kambos

August 8

Wednesday

4th ♊

☽ → ♋ 12:01 am

Color of the day: Brown
Incense of the day: Lilac

Love Magick Divination

On this day, the ancient Romans celebrated the Eve of the Festival of Venus. The night was given over to songs, prayers, and pouring libations in her honor, as well as wild lovemaking. Sorceresses were said to perform magical divination for love and marriage. Love magic is seen as potentially manipulative by modern Witches, but it's possible to use our intuition to see what the goddess of love may have in mind for us.

On this night, place two roses on your altar, and tie the stems together with ribbon (red or pink are best). Light red or pink candles. Place photos or the names of single people whose love lives you want to gain insights about (include yourself if you wish). Stare at each photo and say the person's name, then say:

What will love bring to you?

When you go to bed, rub some perfumed oil on your wrists. Use something earthy and sensual to relax you and conjure thoughts of romance (vetiver, patchouli, rose, amber, or sandalwood are all good). Think of the names and faces of the people on your altar, and with any luck you will dream of them and gain insight into their love lives.

Peg Aloi

NOTES:

August 9
Thursday

4th ♋
☽ v/c 7:21 am

Color of the day: Purple
Incense of the day: Carnation

The Power of the horse

The first horses arrived in Hawaii on this day in 1803. Can you imagine what it must have been like to see them for the first time? As a totem animal, horse brings raw energy and power. It's a symbol of freedom and new journeys. Every different color of horse means something slightly different: white is for purity, black for determination, red for energy, gold for awareness, etc.

It's easy to invite the energies of horse into your life so that you can work with them. Put a picture of a horse on your altar, or wear horse-themed jewelry. If you're able to visit a horse farm or dude ranch, get some firsthand experience. Working with horse builds trust and patience, which is why equine therapy is gaining popularity when it comes to emotional healing.

Charlie Rainbow Wolf

August 10
Friday

4th ♋
☽ → ♌ 12:18 am

Color of the day: Pink
Incense of the day: Violet

Crown of Power Shield

With the sun and moon both in Leo, the "king" of the zodiac, we can create an extra-powerful psychic shield that can be reinforced at any time.

Buy or make a crown (even a paper one will do) and place it on your head. Close your eyes and meditate, visualizing that the crown is glowing with energy. See the energy grow and envelop you like a bubble. Feel as though the crown is a symbol of your total sovereignty; it is your emblem of personal power. The shield of power is strong, solid, and complete. Feel it condense, and affirm it with these words:

Shield of power, my royal crown,
keep me safe from any harm.

From this point on, whenever you feel the need for protection, visualize the crown on your head and feel the magical strength it provides.

Michael Furie

August 11

Saturday

4th ♌

☽ v/c 5:58 am

New Moon 5:58 am

☽ → ♍ 11:59 pm

Color of the day: Blue

Incense of the day: Patchouli

Solar Eclipse

Embracing the Shadow Self

During a solar eclipse, the sun is obscured in shadow. This is a good time to look at our shadow self and do some introspective work. If you can do this meditation at the time of the eclipse, it will work the best. Sit outside under the sun (if possible) during this time period. Close your eyes and envision yourself walking toward your shadow self. Contemplate what about that primal being unnerves you. When you have learned what you can from your shadow self, embrace it. Take the positive qualities of your shadow self with you into the light.

Charlynn Walls

August 12

Sunday

1st ♍

Color of the day: Gold

Incense of the day: Juniper

Bills Are Due Bewitched Money Jar

You just found out your child needs braces and there's a knock in your engine, but the electricity payment is due and your cupboards are bare. Don't we hate it when unexpected expenses creep into our lives? This bewitched money jar just might help. You will need:

- A large glass jar
- A green permanent marker
- Basil leaves
- Some coins
- A green aventurine
- A green drawstring bag

Take a large glass jar and use the marker to draw personal symbols of wealth on it. Now take the basil leaves, coins, and green aventurine and place them in the green drawstring bag. Place the bag in the bottom of the jar. Imagine that for every coin you place in the jar, its value will find its way into your life three times three. Now say:

For every coin I add, may my wealth increase three times three.

Add spare and/or found change daily until the jar is full.

Monica Crosson

NOTES:

August 13
Monday

1st ♍

Color of the day: Lavender
Incense of the day: Lily

International Lefthanders Day

It's International Lefthanders Day. As you may know, the left hand is governed by the right side of the brain, which is more creative and intuitive than the left. This means that we can activate and access our psychic powers simply by writing or drawing with our left hand.

Whether you're usually left-handed or right-handed, try this: Using your right hand, write out a question or issue on which you'd like guidance. Then switch to your left hand and simply write or draw whatever comes up in response, without stopping, trying to make sense of it, or thinking too much about it. (For example, you might ask about a relationship, and then you might draw a raccoon or jot down a poem.) When this feels complete, take a moment to assess what you've written or drawn. How might this apply to your issue? What message is your subconscious and intuitive mind communicating?

Tess Whitehurst

August 14
Tuesday

1st ♍

☽ v/c 12:37 am

☽ → ♎ 12:57 am

Color of the day: Scarlet
Incense of the day: Cedar

Balance Check

Light one black and one white candle. Take a seat and place the candles in front of you. Focus on both candles and take a mental inventory of your life. Do you feel like your life is in balance the best it can be? If so, give thanks and give yourself a virtual pat on the back for achieving and maintaining that balance.

If you feel you are out of whack, spend time meditating and evaluating what is off. We often fall into patterns and don't even notice what is happening. Use this time to think about your work life, family life, other relationships, playtime, etc. Is there something you need to work on? The first step is realizing that something isn't quite right and then investigating to discover exactly what it is. Once you figure out where you are, you can figure out where you need to go next.

Kerri Connor

August 15
Wednesday

1st ♎

Color of the day: White
Incense of the day: Marjoram

Visibility Spell

How often do you feel invisible in your life? Unheard, unnoticed, ignored? How much of this is you being self-conscious and how much of it is other people being oblivious?

Make a list of all the things you truly like about yourself, all the reasons you feel people should notice you, hear you, and see you as you truly are. While doing so, hold a crystal in your left hand. Review the list and then rewrite your self-loving statements as affirmations. Say the affirmations out loud, over and over, projecting the energy into the crystal. Say:

*As the moon grows, as the
sun shines, so let energy flow—
recognition is MINE!*

Keep the crystal on your person in all situations where you wish to be noticed, and repeat the affirmations regularly, until you know them to be true. Be blessed.

Thuri Calafia

August 16
Thursday

1st ♎

☽ v/c 3:56 am

☽ → ♏ 4:54 am

Color of the day: Turquoise
Incense of the day: Mulberry

Shower Cleansing with Citrus

In Hinduism and a variety of tantric paths, lemons and limes are sometimes used to drive away malicious external energy. To take advantage of citric magick, take a lemon and/or lime into the shower with you! Stand skyclad (naked) just outside of the water's reach while you break open each fruit and rub the juice all over your body (these juices also help maintain a nice complexion). You may wish to make small cuts in the fruits before taking them into the shower so that you can open them easily without tools.

As the citrus juices cleanse your physical body, focus negative energies and destructive thoughts into the juice and see them washing down the drain. If you have felt bombarded by external energies lately, see these vibes sticking to the juice and rinsing away. Conclude by showering off and giving thanks to the metaphysical healing powers of the natural world.

Raven Digitalis

August 17
Friday

1st ♏

Color of the day: Coral
Incense of the day: Vanilla

Gettin' Ready for the Weekend

It's been one of those loooong weeks at work. Now it's Friday. You deserve a break. What are your weekend plans?

Before you leave your office, make sure your workspace is clean and tidy. You probably have elemental symbols (a rock, a shell, a feather, a red crayon) on one of your shelves. While you're tidying up, lay them in their proper directions and cast a tiny, private circle. Think about what you accomplished this week: projects begun or completed, meetings attended, people networked, problems solved, etc. Say these words, either aloud or in your mind:

Gettin' ready for the weekend,

I've had a busy week.

Gettin' ready for the weekend,

It's pleasure now I seek!

Build a tiny yet strong cone of power (which looks like a tiny tornado, not destructive but beneficial) and send it to your weekend destination. Turn off your computer, turn out the lights, and go home.

Barbara Ardinger

August 18

Saturday

1st ♏

2nd Quarter 3:49 am

☽ v/c 11:07 am

☽ → ♐ 12:45 pm

Color of the day: Brown

Incense of the day: Sage

A Charm for Patience

Who among us couldn't use a little patience? This charm will help you work toward that end.

Use a handkerchief or a piece of cotton fabric—choose blue, gray, or white if possible. Write the word "Patience" on the cloth. Top with a few hawthorn berries, chamomile leaves, or rose petals. Fold the cloth around the contents four times and pin closed with a large safety pin. Tie a string or ribbon around the bundle and pin, fastening it with four square knots. Last but not least, link four paper clips together in a chain, then fasten the chain to the bundle. Repeat:

Patience fleeting, patience how?

Give me practice with patience now!

Keep this charm with you to help you be patient, or give it to someone else who would benefit from it. Undoing it would take some work; thus, patience is encouraged.

Susan Pesznecker

 August 19

Sunday

2nd ♐

Color of the day: Amber

Incense of the day: Almond

Invisibility Spell

On this day in 1692 in Salem, Massachusetts, five more people were hanged as witches: George Burroughs, George Jacobs, Martha Carrier, John Proctor, and John Willard. We're fortunate to be living in a time and place where we are more free to practice our faith, though it may not always be tolerated by all. If you ever feel vulnerable about your beliefs, here's something that might help to make you more invisible.

This spell won't make you disappear, but it will make you less noticeable. Take a deep breath, and as you do, imagine your aura getting smaller and smaller and smaller, until it's just hugging your body. Exhale slowly and repeat these words:

Keep me strong, keep me wise,

Shield me from unwelcome eyes.

While this spell will not fix everything, it will help you to pass less noticeably among people who don't share your beliefs and yet still be recognizable to those who do.

Charlie Rainbow Wolf

August 20

Monday

2nd ♐

☽ v/c 7:47 pm

Color of the day: Silver
Incense of the day: Rosemary

Persistence Divination

Today is the birthday of the notable yet controversial journalist Connie Chung. Chung's overall approach was very gentle, but she became known for a quality of persistence on particularly pressing and controversial questions during interviews. Whether her persistence was appropriate in each case is a topic of wide debate; however, in the proper context, persistence is a quality worthy of admiration.

In honor of persistence, get out your preferred divination tool today and ask a question regarding yourself that has been particularly tough for you to deal with. Be prepared to face the answers you get, and persist with a follow-up question to gain more information and hopefully some traction toward a solution.

Consider your interaction with your divination tools to be a conversation, back and forth, much like an interview. If you do not feel you are being objective, you can work with a friend. That person can either dialogue results with you or assist in performing divination.

Blake Octavian Blair

August 21

Tuesday

2nd ♐

☽ → ♑ 12:00 am

Color of the day: Maroon
Incense of the day: Geranium

Looking Back to Look Forward

It is said that what doesn't kill us makes us stronger. My "clean date" is August 22, 1990. That was the first time I got through the entire day without getting high after many years of addiction.

I've been clean a long time now, but every year on August 21, I look back and remember what that day held for me. I revisit the desperation, fear, and sickness I felt then. Remembering how bad it was when I finally hit bottom has helped motivate me to continually choose to stay clean and sober. I look backward so I never lose sight of the emotions that made me willing to do almost anything to change my life.

Call to mind a difficult experience from your past. Sink into the depth of feelings associated with it. Now turn your eyes toward the future, letting that pain be your guide as you travel.

Dallas Jennifer Cobb

August 22
Wednesday

2nd ♑

Color of the day: Yellow
Incense of the day: Bay laurel

Water Music

Seeing, hearing, and experiencing water in its natural state—falling from the sky or rolling in the waves of the ocean—is not always possible. But water as an elemental power exists everywhere, and we can tap into its energy through music.

French composer Claude Debussy was able to imitate the melody of water with the piano. Today, on his birthday, use his music to enhance a water-element meditation. Listen to Debussy's "Deux Arabesques L. 66— No. 1 Andante con moto" (available for free on YouTube and Spotify). See the notes as water—falling like rain, tripping over stones, flowing in a rocky bed. Let the melody guide what you see. Hint: Keep the piece on loop so that you can continue or repeat the meditation for as long as you need.

Natalie Zaman

 ## August 23
Thursday

2nd ♑

☉ → ♍ 12:09 am
☽ v/c 10:19 am
☽ → ♒ 12:56 pm

Color of the day: Green
Incense of the day: Balsam

Random Acts of Inspirational Kindness

While it's true that performing random acts of kindness can create beneficial karma for the giver, the most important thing is that they help brighten other people's day. As a magickal and spiritual being, you have the opportunity (if not the responsibility) to spread goodness however you are able.

Take a few moments today to write inspirational messages on twenty-three slips of paper (twenty-three is considered a number of "chaos"). The messages you write can be the same on each slip, such as an inspirational quote or a rhyming spell, or each message can be different, based on your intuition or even any divination you may do for each slip.

Feel free to decorate each piece of paper with fun symbols or stickers while remembering that you are helping deliver messages to inspire people.

Leave these papers to be found at random in public places, trusting in the divine process of synchronicity.

Raven Digitalis

NOTES:

 August 24

Friday

2nd ♒

Color of the day: Purple
Incense of the day: Yarrow

Early harvest Observation

This day marks the Icelandic festival of Freyfaxi, the time of harvest in ancient Iceland. This festival is celebrated with a sacrifice (blot) to Freyr (brother of Freya; both represent fertility and fruitfulness) and a grand feast from the goods of the harvest.

This is a time when many wonderful fruits and vegetables come into season. Get one or more of your favorites from a local farmers' market or store (or maybe you or a friend has a garden or some berry bushes), and place an arrangement on your altar: maybe a bowl of berries, peaches, early apples, or some garlic or herbs. Give thanks to the gods for this abundant gift from the earth. Prepare a dish from this harvest, and when you eat it, know you are being nourished by the earth and the people who tend her life-giving plants.

Harvest is a potent time to reflect on the abundance we have in our lives. Replace the produce on your altar regularly during this season to remind you of the abundance and gifts in your life that nourish you.

Peg Aloi

August 25

Saturday

2nd ♒

☽ v/c 12:39 am

Color of the day: Black
Incense of the day: Pine

Communication Breakdown Spell

Do you ever wonder if you're being heard? Maybe your partner just doesn't seem to understand your needs. Maybe it's a miscommunication on the job. How about the kids? Yeah, I know how it is.

If communication has broken down in your life, use the element of air to build it back up. This spell works well on a breezy day.

You will need a piece of paper and a pen, a white tealight candle, and a fire-safe container.

Write everything you need to communicate on the paper. Light the tealight candle and catch a corner of the paper on fire. Place the burning paper in the fire-safe container and let it burn to ash. Then lift the container and say:

*Element of air, send my
words to every ear*

*So that communication
can now be clear.*

*With the power of wind
and breath and song,*

*Let the magick hold, my
message strong.*

Blow the ash into the breeze.

Monica Crosson

NOTES:

August 26

Sunday

2nd ≈

☽ → ♓ 1:32 am

Full Moon 7:56 am

Color of the day: Orange
Incense of the day: Frankincense

Mending Fences Spell

With this full moon, and Lughnasadh so recently past, personal sacrifice is highlighted. If we've fallen prey to the crankiness that the dog days of summer can bring, we probably have some fences to mend, whether with a friend or lover or even ourselves.

For this spell, take a pale blue pillar candle and inscribe it with all the loving words and symbols you can think of that speak to you and the other person. Let your heart be filled with the love and affection you feel for this person. Anoint the candle with lavender oil to induce peace and harmony, and speak the words of apology and love you feel you need to say to the other. Light the candle and say:

Let there be peace between us,
always, in love and in truth.
Blessed be, (name of person).

Then follow up by meeting with the person and speaking the words you just spoke to their spirit.

Thuri Calafia

August 27

Monday

3rd ♓

Color of the day: White
Incense of the day: Narcissus

Leaf Pressing

As the Wheel of the Year begins to turn toward autumn, we often contemplate where the summer went. If you want to keep some energy from summer, collect several leaves or plants from your area that are still vibrant, and find a large book that you can use. Take and place the leaves or plants in wax paper and then place them between the pages of the book. Put the book in a cool, dry area that is away from direct sunlight. You can place additional books on top if added weight is needed. After the leaves have dried, you can use them to add a bit of summer energy to your magickal workings!

Charlynn Walls

August 28

Tuesday

3rd ♓

☽ v/c 9:54 am

☽ → ♈ 12:35 pm

Color of the day: Gray
Incense of the day: Bayberry

Candle Magic for Safe Travel

If you are going on a long trip or just want to ensure your safety during a work commute, this spell can help. Hold an unlit white candle in your hands and visualize your trip. See a bubble of protection surrounding you. Set the candle on a table and light it. As the flame leaps up, again strongly visualize being protected on your journey and say:

Safe in my travels I will be,
through each step of the way;
secured and empowered, of
worries I'm free, and surrounded
by magic to protect each day.

Snuff out the candle and watch the smoke leaving the glowing wick. As the glow fades, see the last puff of smoke released from the candle as carrying out your magic to bring it to manifestation.

Michael Furie

August 29

Wednesday

3rd ♈

Color of the day: Brown
Incense of the day: Lilac

Protection from Nightmares

Stress in our lives can produce unpleasant dreams and disrupt our sleep cycles, which can negatively impact our health. Lavender is calming and can help prolong sleep and ease the stressful thoughts that can lead to nightmares.

Place a bowl of saltwater beneath your bed, and before you go to sleep, place a few drops of lavender essential oil on the surface of the water. Do this each night until dreams improve.

You can also put a sprig of lavender or a lavender sachet under your pillow. Before sleeping, think back over the day's events in reverse order. This can help to reduce mental stress, which can sometimes cause nightmares to occur as our brain attempts to problem-solve during sleep.

Try not to obsess over anything. Briefly acknowledge problems and tell yourself you will "sleep on it." Breathe deeply, and briefly tense and release each set of muscles, from head to toe. Refresh the lavender oil before bed to help you fall asleep gently and peacefully.

Peg Aloi

August 30

Thursday

3rd ♈

☽ v/c 7:04 pm

☽ → ♉ 9:30 pm

Color of the day: Crimson
Incense of the day: Clove

Pay Mother Earth Ritual

At this time of year, Mother Earth once again shares her bounty with us. Even though we mistreat her, she still gives back to us. In this ritual, we will "pay" her back for a change.

You'll need four barley grains. Barley is used because at one time it was used as currency, and the number four represents the seasons. Perform this ritual in a garden, field, or soil-filled pot. Press the grains of barley into the soil and say:

Mother Earth,

I thank you for spring, when we plant and growth begins.

I thank you for summer, when the fields ripen.

I thank you for autumn, when you share the harvest.

I thank you for winter, when you prepare to nourish us again.

Mother Earth, thank you for sustaining us.

After this ritual, unexpected good fortune may come to you. Mother Earth knows you've shown your appreciation for her.

James Kambos

NOTES:

August 31
Friday

3rd ♉

Color of the day: Rose
Incense of the day: Alder

Name Your Fame

While some of us desire fame in the usual sense of being a movie star or a rock legend, a large number of us would prefer to be known for something more local and less flashy, such as our cookie recipes, our computer programming prowess, or our mad tarot skills. But make no mistake: we may not need to win an Oscar, but we *all* want to be seen and appreciated for something. It's how we're made.

So today, light a red pillar candle, burn some cinnamon incense, and brew a cup of cinnamon tea. Relax, center yourself, and take some time to list all the ways you'd most like to be known and seen in the world. Phrase your desires in the present tense, as if they're already true. Fold the paper and place it under the candle. Allow the candle to burn at intervals all the way down.

Tess Whitehurst

NOTES:

September

The equinox happens toward the end of this month, heralding the beginning of autumn in the Northern Hemisphere and the start of spring in the Southern Hemisphere. An equinox happens when the sun crosses the celestial equator, an imaginary line in the sky not unlike our Earth's own equator. It's on the equinox that the sun rises due east and sets due west. This is why people often go to famous landmarks to watch the rising or setting of the sun on the equinoxes and solstices. In our ever-changing world, it's nice to know there are at least some constants!

Astrologically, the autumnal equinox is when the sun sign of Libra begins. It's fitting, as this is the time when day and night are of equal length, and Libra is the sign of the scales. The full moon that corresponds with this event is called the Harvest Moon or the Corn Moon. The few days around the equinox and the full moon bring a period in which everything is ripening and full of energy. It all seems to be coming into fullness, preparing either for the coming of winter or the start of the growing season.

Charlie Rainbow Wolf

September 1
Saturday

3rd ♉

Color of the day: Gray
Incense of the day: Sandalwood

Protective Runes

There are times when a little extra protection is warranted, such as when a person lives in an area with a high crime rate or someone is in a war zone. A good way to help ensure a loved one's safety is to add a protective rune to their clothing.

Begin by creating a sacred space where you can focus on your intent of safety and protection. Take a jacket or other item of clothing that the person wears often, and add a protective rune to the inside of it. You can do this by sewing the rune onto the inside of the item of clothing. Don't worry about how it looks, because you are putting it in a place that cannot be seen. As you work, say:

This cloth shall protect you.
As I will it, so shall it be.

Charlynn Walls

September 2
Sunday

3rd ♉
☽ v/c 1:56 am
☽ → ♊ 4:02 am
4th Quarter 10:37 pm

Color of the day: Gold
Incense of the day: Hyacinth

Love Yourself

Today is a day to celebrate you and the love you have for yourself. If you don't feel like you have much love for yourself, today you can work on that.

If you do feel love for yourself, feel the appreciation and pride of your own self-love. Light a pink candle and either sit in front of a mirror or use a hand mirror. Stare into the mirror. Stare into yourself. Look deep into your own eyes. What do you see? If negative thoughts creep into your mind, dismiss them and send them on their way. This time is for positive thoughts only. What are your good qualities? Look at more than just your physical qualities. Look deep into yourself. What makes you a good and special person? Celebrate those qualities. Be proud that you have them. Thank your deities for making you the person that you are.

Kerri Connor

September 3
Monday

4th ♊

Color of the day: Gray
Incense of the day: Neroli

Labor Day

Invoking the Divine

L ong weekends stretch out
luxuriously, like a time warp.
We can slow down and savor them.
But for many of us, this is the last
long weekend of summer. Tomorrow
the kids go back to school, and we
will have to shift gears suddenly and
get up to speed quickly. Today, let's
choose to invoke the divine. Let's let
go of the need to control, make, or
do. Let's release worry and anxiety,
and just trust.

Grab a paper and pen. Taking no
more than five minutes, write down
everything you are worried about.
What you need to do and remember.
Lists. Tomorrow's stuff. Your fears
and anxiety.

When everything is recorded, fold
the paper. Place it on your altar (in a
box, if you have one) and say:

I invoke the divine. I release
these worries to Higher Order.
Goddess, this is in your hands.

Now go out and enjoy this spectacu-
lar last hurrah of summer.

Dallas Jennifer Cobb

 ## September 4
Tuesday

4th ♊

☽ v/c 2:37 am
☽ → ♋ 8:03 am

Color of the day: Black
Incense of the day: Cinnamon

Emotional Healing Bath

T oday is a good day to comfort,
soothe, and draw out old pain
related to love or family relationships
with the element of water. Draw a
warm bath and add the following:

- 1 cup Epsom salt
- ¼ cup baking soda
- 1 moonstone (that has been
cleansed in running water)
- 13 drops essential oil of lavender

Light a white candle. Stand outside
the bath and direct your palms toward
the water. See the bathwater filled
with bright, silvery-white light. Say:

Great Mother Goddess and Lady
of the Moon, thank you for filling
this water with light that heals
my heart, draws out old pain,
and brings comfort to my soul.

Soak for twenty to forty minutes, feeling the old pain draining out of you
and allowing yourself to relax deeply
and fully. Make sure to drink plenty of
water to replenish your fluids and help
wash away old toxins.

Tess Whitehurst

September 5

Wednesday

4th ♋

Color of the day: White
Incense of the day: Marjoram

Laundry Day Spellcrafting

Washing laundry can seem like a monotonous chore, but putting a little spiritual intention into even the most mundane activity can make things fun while keeping the good vibes flowing.

Add a few drops of pure lavender essential oil to your load of laundry. After the clothes are dry, as you fold each item, put a dab of lavender oil on it while focusing on the plentiful metaphysical qualities of lavender, which include relaxation, peace, mental focus, balance, sensuality, and protection. You may wish to create a little chant to say with each dab. This process serves to enchant your garments and lend them a metaphysical boost for many days down the road.

You may also wish to experiment with different essential oils depending on their properties, or dilute your oils if you are sensitive to odors. Just be sure not to use "fragrance" oils because of their toxicity.

Raven Digitalis

 September 6

Thursday

4th ♋

☽ v/c 8:43 am
☽ → ♌ 9:54 am

Color of the day: Turquoise
Incense of the day: Nutmeg

Kitchen Witch's Canning Blessing

September arrives on golden light. The air is scented with apple and leaves begin to turn. This is the time of year when the song of autumn truly begins to tug at our souls.

During this time, many of us are busily putting up food for the winter. Here is a simple canning blessing to enchant your winter stores. You will need a wooden spoon and some of your preserved food: a couple jars of jam, dried fruit or beans, frozen fruits or vegetables, etc.

Hold the wooden spoon over your newly preserved food, and imagine the warmth and nourishment you are providing for you and your loved ones. Now say:

Bless all that is created to nourish our bodies.

Bless all that is created to nourish our souls.

Bless all that is created to nourish our minds.

Blessed be.

Monica Crosson

September 7
Friday

4th ♌

Color of the day: Pink
Incense of the day: Rose

Into the Deep Earth

The time of the waning moon, especially just before the new moon, is an ideal time for introspection and inner work. This meditation brings an awareness of the land and provides an opportunity to release stress and worry.

Close your eyes. Envision a cave in front of you. Walk into the cave and keep going further through the darkness until you come to a clearing lit by a soft inner glow. Sit down in this clearing, feeling the land beneath you. Look up and see where the light is coming from, a million little lights glowing above— the stars inside the earth. Now is the time to connect and release. Feel the security of the earth and let go of anything that troubles you, knowing the energy will be recycled by the land. When you are ready to end the meditation, walk out of the cave and open your eyes.

Michael Furie

September 8

Saturday

4th ♌

☽ v/c 9:31 am

☽ → ♍ 10:29 am

Color of the day: Blue
Incense of the day: Rue

Old-School Divination Spell

Today marks the anniversary of the founding of the Theosophical Society by Helena Blavatsky and a group of other occultists. Blavatsky's books, including *Isis Unveiled*, were important influences in the early days of the modern occult revival movement. Occultism permeates Wicca and other Pagan traditions, particularly in divination practices. One of the most tried-and-true divinatory methods is the tarot. This spell will help you connect with the tarot's wisdom.

Take your tarot deck and meditate on an important question. Choose one card. Study it intently and make a drawing utilizing the symbols of the card, but place yourself (or your name) in the drawing too. Put this paper on your altar to charge it, and then by your bedside before bedtime. Meditate on the card's symbolism before you sleep. Keep a notebook and pen by the bed in case you have insights about your dreams upon awakening. Do this each night for three days, choosing a different card each time. Tarot symbolism in dreams is considered very magically potent and significant.

Peg Aloi

NOTES:

September 9

Sunday

4th ♍

New Moon 2:01 pm

Color of the day: Amber

Incense of the day: Marigold

A New Moon Spell

This new moon occurs when the sun is in Virgo, which makes it a good time to start any magical work having to do with health, diet, nutrition, career, business, or education. To help you achieve your goal, try this method of spellwork.

Begin by writing down your goal on paper. Place this on your altar. On one side of the paper place an orange candle for success, and on the other side place a royal-blue candle for expansion. Don't light them yet.

For three nights, starting tonight, read or chant your goal aloud. On the third night, read it again and then light each candle to release the spell's power. Let them burn awhile, then snuff them out. Keep the paper and repeat this ritual if you wish during the full moon. When you attain your goal, discard the paper.

James Kambos

September 10

Monday

1st ♍

☽ v/c 11:12 am

☽ → ♎ 11:20 am

Color of the day: Lavender

Incense of the day: Hyssop

Rosh hashanah

Clear Dreams Spell

To make a Clear Dreaming Balm, place about 1 teaspoon each of cinnamon, frankincense, and rose petals in a small slow cooker or glass double boiler, and add enough coconut oil (about 2 tablespoons) to cover the herbs when melted. Cook for 3 to 3½ hours in the double boiler or 13 hours in the slow cooker to completely infuse the herbs into the coconut oil. Strain, reheat, and add a few shavings of beeswax, plus a few drops each of sandalwood and lavender oil. While making this balm, chant:

May my dreams be clear,

May my dreams be strong.

Let clarity reign all the night long.

Place a small amount of balm over your third eye as you're getting into bed, while thinking hard about the question you're seeking an answer to. Repeat the chant until sleep comes. Blessed dreams!

Thuri Calafia

September 11

Tuesday

1st ♎

☽ v/c 6:58 pm

Color of the day: Scarlet
Incense of the day: Ylang-ylang

Islamic New Year

Let There Be Peace

For many people, this is a day of remembrance and mourning. Countless lives were touched back in 2001 when the Twin Towers came down. With today's waxing Libra moon, it's a good day to pause and remember those whose lives were taken or changed forever, and offer up a prayer for peace.

To do this ritual, simply light a white candle and repeat the following words:

May peace be before me.

May peace be around me.

May peace shine throughout me.

May I walk in peace.

Send peace now to others.

Send peace to all mothers.

Let us love like brothers.

Let us walk in peace.

Pinch the candle out and get on with your day. You might even want to use this as a start for a year of peace, where you send out the prayer every morning to bring comfort to all those who are grieving or in turmoil.

Charlie Rainbow Wolf

NOTES:

September 12

Wednesday

1st ♎

☽ → ♏ 2:15 pm

Color of the day: Topaz
Incense of the day: Lavender

happy Birthday

When a friend of yours has a birthday, give them a spell along with their gift. First think about what this friend means to you. Think about things you've done together. Give your friend a birthday agate.

Look online or in a book for information about the magical properties of stones to determine which kind of agate is best for this friend. The energies of agates include longevity, healing, and protection. For your friend's birthday, select a gorgeous agate. Holding the agate, visualize your friend. See your friend as healthy, productive, and happy. Say:

Hinkety, pinkety, play,

Today's (friend's name's) natal day!

Good health I send (him/her)

And happy life.

Hinkety, pinkety, plurn,

Happy solar return!

Give the agate to your friend and teach them the spell so they can pay it forward.

Barbara Ardinger

 September 13

Thursday

1st ♏

Color of the day: White
Incense of the day: Apricot

harvest Bounty

Even though the harvest season is starting to wind down, now is the time to give thanks for everything that has come in so far. Mabon is just around the corner and is known as the second harvest. Be sure to pick offerings for your Mabon celebration from your garden. Even if you don't garden, you do benefit from the garden and agricultural trades of others, so be sure to pick up some type of offering.

Take inventory of the other "harvests" in your life as well. Give thanks for the prosperity you have. Even though you are thankful, you may feel as if you don't have everything you need. This happens to us a lot—we feel like we don't have enough money, enough food, enough clothes, enough love. Take this day to feel truly thankful and appreciative for what you do have.

Kerri Connor

September 14

Friday

1st ♏

☽ v/c 4:54 am

☽ → ♐ 8:45 pm

Color of the day: Coral
Incense of the day: Mint

Extra Strength Attraction Spell

Today, the aspects are excellent to do a spell on yourself to incite passion and become absolutely irresistible to others. The effect should last throughout the weekend. But be careful with this one, okay? It's no joke.

Light a deep red pillar candle and some vanilla incense in your bathroom and draw a warm bath. Add two drops of ylang-ylang and three drops of sandalwood essential oils to the water, and stir with your right hand in an infinity symbol as you chant the following three times:

I flow like water, I burn like fire.
I attract lust, I attract desire.

Soak by candlelight for at least forty minutes. Dry off and anoint your lower belly with a mixture of ylang-ylang and sandalwood (dilute with a carrier oil if you have sensitive skin).

Tess Whitehurst

 September 15

Saturday

1st ♐

Color of the day: Black
Incense of the day: Ivy

Signed, Sealed, and Delivered

Words are magic. They make ideas real and tangible, and they put the process of change in motion. They are simple but powerful. So too is your signature—your personal symbol of agreement that is a potent seal for any spell, wish, or desire.

As summer comes to a close, think about what you want to come to pass by the year's end. Write it all down. When you're finished, read it aloud. Then sign your name. Feel the power of determination and success flowing through the pen. You will make these things happen.

As your wishes come to pass, tear off a piece of the paper and burn it—save the portion with your signature for last. Use your signature to seal any spell or written magical work.

Natalie Zaman

September 16

Sunday

1st ♐

☽ v/c 7:15 pm

2nd Quarter 7:15 pm

Color of the day: Yellow
Incense of the day: Heliotrope

Gratitude Talisman

With pen or pencil, write "Gratitude" on a piece of paper. Then make a list of everything and everyone you are currently grateful for. Be expansive! For instance, the fact that you wake up each morning is, without a doubt, worthy of gratitude. So is that nice view out the kitchen window. So are the people you love.

When you're finished, roll or fold the paper and tie it with a yellow or gold ribbon—the colors of gold, sunshine, and abundance. Offer this prayer while holding the paper in your hands:

O, (insert deity name), help me be grateful for the blessings in my life.

For even with any challenges I may face each day, it is still a beautiful world.

You've now created a gratitude talisman. Hold it in your hands and meditate (or open it and read it) when you need a boost, feeling its energies rejuvenate your spirits.

Susan Pesznecker

September 17

Monday

2nd ♐

☽ → ♑ 7:07 am

Color of the day: Ivory
Incense of the day: Clary sage

Click and Be Grateful

With any luck, your September routines are up and running. Now that you're back from vacation, work has resumed and schedules have been established. Kids are settling into waking up early and going to school. Lunches get packed and homework gets done.

It feels so busy. It has required a few weeks of focused effort to get everyone moving again after summer. And when we exert so much effort, sometimes we forget to be thankful.

Today, whenever you hear a "click," pause and be grateful. The kids run out of the house and the door clicks: be thankful for your home, your kids' health, and everyone's safety. You shut the car door, or the bus door closes behind you: be grateful for freedom, mobility, infrastructure, and transportation. The door at your workplace closes: give thanks for good work, income, and opportunity.

With each click today, pause, look around, and give thanks. You are blessed. Life is good. Say:

Thank you.

Dallas Jennifer Cobb

September 18

Tuesday

2nd ♑

Color of the day: Red
Incense of the day: Ginger

Blessing for Medicine

No matter how healthy we may be, at some point we'll have to take medicine. Whether it's doctor-prescribed medication or cough syrup from the store, a bit of blessing magic can help to align our bodies with healing energy and also try to minimize potential side effects from the medicine.

To begin, hold the bottle in your hands and visualize yourself in a healthy state. Mentally send white light into the medicine and say:

Vital medicine I hereby bless, to
restore my body, good health defend;
diminish all that would cause stress,
absorbing only what will soothe
and mend; for highest good, by free
will, let this magic be fulfilled.

The medicine should then be taken as prescribed.

Michael Furie

September 19

Wednesday

2nd ♑

☽ v/c 1:10 pm

☽ → ♒ 7:52 pm

Color of the day: Brown
Incense of the day: Honeysuckle

Yom Kippur

Treasure Attraction Spell

Today is the much-loved pop-culture holiday Talk Like a Pirate Day. Since we'll all be talking like pirates, why not work a little treasure spell for abundance? We shall aim to acquire our treasure by more admirable means than those used by many pirates.

Get a sheet of paper or a piece of poster board, a pair of scissors, and some glue. Find images of what you consider to be treasure online, in old magazines, or in ads. Remember, treasure is not simply monetary; abundance and treasure come in many forms. You may want to use images of a home, favorite foods, animals and pets, books, craft supplies, or anything you perceive as treasure! Don't forget (for fun and to link up our energetic theme) an image of a pirate's treasure chest! Hang the finished product near your altar. To charge, burn an orange candle down safely while envisioning your goal manifesting for the highest good.

Blake Octavian Blair

September 20

Thursday

2nd ♒

Color of the day: Crimson
Incense of the day: Carnation

A Spell for Insomnia

If you have had a particularly difficult time falling asleep or staying asleep recently, consider doing some spellcraft to aid the situation.

Before bed, try meditating for a full ten minutes in total silence by sitting up in your bed and clearing your mind to the best of your ability. Count your breaths. As you do this, burn a violet/purple candle that has been anointed with pure lavender essential oil. You may also wish to inscribe the candle with little images of closed eyes and ZZZs. Extinguish the candle before lying down for slumber.

In addition to this candle magick, you may wish to stitch your own lavender-stuffed sleepytime pillow or stuffed animal to sleep with. Finally, if your insomnia is ongoing, consider speaking with a sleep specialist or trying some natural short-term remedies for restfulness, such as tryptophan or melatonin. If you are taking any other medications, be sure to do some research (or check with your doctor) to ensure that nothing will negatively interact.

Raven Digitalis

September 21

Friday

2nd ♒

☽ v/c 1:13 pm

Color of the day: White
Incense of the day: Thyme

UN International Day of Peace

Day of Divination

Today marks the International Day of Peace, a time when countries all over the world offer events to promote peace and justice. The image of the scales of justice (the symbol of Libra) is fitting for this day, since the sun will enter that sign tomorrow at the autumnal equinox. You may choose to participate in a demonstration or perhaps take part in a quieter, more personal ritual today.

This calendar date is also traditional for performing divination in old Europe. One German tradition describes young girls making fortune-telling wreaths out of straw and evergreen to mark the midpoint between summer and winter. This middle season is a potent time for reflection. Surrounded by beauty and abundant growth, we prepare for the darker days ahead by harvesting abundance and deciding what will nurture us going forward.

This is a good time to do divination work for the changing seasonal tide. Using your favorite method (runes, tarot, I Ching, etc.), tap into this in-between time between light and dark, reflecting on balance, justice, and peace and how they affect your path in life.

Peg Aloi

NOTES:

September 22
Saturday

2nd ♒

☽ → ♓ 8:27 am

☉ → ♎ 9:54 pm

Color of the day: Indigo
Incense of the day: Sage

Mabon – Fall Equinox

Finding Balance

Mabon is observed on an equinox, a time when there are equal parts of light and day. It is the perfect time to reassess and work toward balance in all parts of your life.

Set up your altar to reflect the harvest. Place a black and a white candle on opposite sides of the altar, and place a piece of parchment in between them. On this paper, write down the aspects of your life that you feel need to be brought into balance. As you contemplate those aspects, light the candles and say:

As day and night are now in balance,
so to let my life find balance.

Charlynn Walls

September 23
Sunday

2nd ♓

Color of the day: Gold
Incense of the day: Eucalyptus

Fog-Be-Gone Bath

I don't know about you, but I have a very busy life. Between the farm, writing, working, and supporting the needs of my family of five, some days I'm not only physically exhausted but mentally exhausted as well.

Here's a relaxing way to clear a foggy, exhausted mind. You will need:

• A few yellow candles

• Bathtub

• Essential oil blend: 4 drops lemongrass and 2 drops rosemary added to 2 ounces of your favorite carrier oil (such as a light olive oil or, my favorite, fractionated coconut oil)

Take your candles into the bathroom and light them. Fill the bathtub with warm water and add a few drops of your essential oil blend to the tub.

Get in the tub, and as you relax, imagine the water washing away the clutter from your life. Take in the clarifying scent of the oil. Imagine your mind clear and focused. See yourself alert and at ease with your daily tasks. When finished, dab a little more of the oil on your temples.

Monica Crosson

September 24

Monday

2nd ♓

☽ v/c 1:26 am

☽ → ♈ 7:04 pm

Full Moon 10:52 pm

Color of the day: Silver
Incense of the day: Lily

Sukkot begins

Feast of Booths

Our Jewish friends celebrate Sukkot to commemorate forty years of wandering in the desert and living in booths—little huts— before they arrived in their Promised Land. The people are commanded to celebrate this holiday. Let's celebrate with them.

With a piece of your favorite fresh fruit in hand, find a shady spot under a tree. Cast your circle with you and the tree in the north. Look in each direction and imagine weary travelers coming home. Say these words:

Gods and goddesses of all peoples,

Bless our homes.

Bless our goings and our comings.

*Bless our people that we
may live in peace.*

Bless our families that we may prosper.

*Bless our harvest that there
may always be enough.*

*Bless our sad days, our happy
days, our festivals.*

May we celebrate together every year.

As you eat your piece of fresh fruit, think about people who come and go and finally find their homes. And now ... celebrate!

Barbara Ardinger

NOTES:

September 25

Tuesday

3rd ♈

Color of the day: Maroon
Incense of the day: Cedar

A Bittersweet Protection Charm

Bittersweet isn't just an attractive fall decoration, it's also a powerful protective herb. But to be effective, it must be hidden. Here is a protection charm you can make for your home.

You'll need a six-inch square of blue fabric, three bittersweet berries, a pinch each of nutmeg and cinnamon, and some garden twine. Lay the fabric flat. In the center of the square, place all the herbal ingredients. Bring the corners of the fabric together and tie securely with the garden twine. Leave the ends of the twine long enough so you can make a loop to hang the charm with.

Hang your charm bag in a closet, attic, or cellar, or place one under your bed. If you can, make more than one. After you've placed your charm bags, charge them by saying:

Sacred herbs, protect my
family and home.

Dark spirits, retreat, leave us alone.

James Kambos

September 26
Wednesday

3rd ♈

☽ v/c 6:28 am

Color of the day: Yellow
Incense of the day: Bay laurel

Magical Shawl

I've found that the right magical adornment helps create magical atmosphere and space. But I like to keep it simple, and a magical shawl is a super way to do that.

Purchase 1½ yards of fabric—your choice of color, texture, and pattern. (Hint: at this pre-Samhain time of year, fabric stores are loaded with materials in magical colors and patterns!)

Drape the fabric around your shoulders and determine the length and width needed to make a pleasant fit. Using scissors, trim the fabric to fit your measurements. Finish the edges by turning and sewing a simple hem, or, if you don't sew, create a hem with iron-on fusible webbing. Even simpler? Use pinking shears to "pink" an edge.

Bless your shawl by placing it over your shoulders and saying:

*May this magical shawl ease my
way into the magical realm.*

Charge it on your altar or in sunlight or moonlight for twenty-four hours.

Use your shawl when you read about, study, or work magic. Each time it settles around your shoulders, you'll feel yourself slip into magical space.

Susan Pesznecker

NOTES:

September 27

Thursday

3rd ♈

☽ → ♉ 3:16 am

Color of the day: Purple
Incense of the day: Mulberry

Safe Space Spell

Whatever it is that's making you feel unsafe, first do everything in the mundane world you can (lock doors, go stay with a friend, etc.) to help the magic along. Cast your circle and call the quarters in your usual way. Then take a pale blue pillar candle and, while visualizing yourself completely safe and calm and in the presence of your own personal deities, carve runes, letters, or other symbols to represent the elements of your visualization. Dress the candle with lavender oil from top to bottom (to pull in energies) while chanting these words:

I am safe and well at peace.

I have all of my allies with me.

My mind is at rest, my heart is at ease.

Only love may enter, so mote it be!

Continue chanting as you place the candle in a fireproof dish, and when ready, light the candle. Visualize the light from the flame extending outward, all around you, filling your magic circle with light and peace. Be blessed.

Thuri Calafia

September 28

Friday

3rd ♉

☽ v/c 6:36 pm

Color of the day: Pink
Incense of the day: Orchid

Freedom from Hunger Spell

Today is Freedom from Hunger Day. The day was established to bring awareness to the issue of world hunger and to call people to action through community and other events. In our busy lives, we often forget that hunger exists on a local level as well. This spell will help you be part of the solution through both magick and real-world action.

Gather a small candle and an item to donate to your local food pantry. Place both upon your altar and light the candle. Envision the light surrounding your altar, surrounding the donation item, and surrounding and expanding to even greater areas, thereby illuminating the issue of world hunger and offering healing light. When finished, let the candle safely burn out or extinguish it, then donate the item and keep doing your part.

Blake Octavian Blair

September 29

Saturday

3rd ♉

☽ → ♊ 9:26 am

Color of the day: Brown
Incense of the day: Magnolia

Gemini Moon

The waning moon enters the sign of Gemini today. This is good for socializing, but you may feel more introverted than usual. Reading, research, and other intellectual pursuits are favored. Just make sure you're not spreading yourself too thin. You'll need to stay focused; there's some superficial energy here that can be distracting if you let it. If you get derailed, your long-term goals could be delayed. Here's a quick spell to help you stay focused.

You'll need a black or dark green candle. Light it and focus on the flame. Say the following words:

Candle flame that's shining bright,

Help me focus with your light.

Let me not distracted be,

Long-term goals I want to see.

Pinch out the candle flame. Remember your goals and learn how to say no to any interruptions so that you stay focused on what you really want out of life.

Charlie Rainbow Wolf

September 30

Sunday

3rd ♊

☽ v/c 11:38 am

Color of the day: Orange
Incense of the day: Juniper

Sukkot ends

Carrot Bundle for Prosperity

At the end of September, women in Scotland would go out into the hills to dig up wild carrots, then give them out in bunches of three tied with red ribbon as tokens of prosperity and plenty in the coming year. (Split roots were especially lucky!) Considering their shape, carrots are talismans for fertility and virility. They also repel negativity. As winter looms, create a simple charm reminiscent of this old way.

Bind three carrots with red ribbon or yarn, then knot it three times. Seal the magic with these words:

A root for health,

A root for wealth,

A root that's just for me.

Upon my dish,

Grant my wish,

My will, so mote it be!

Eat the carrots to imbibe the charm. If you want to add a bit of passion and decadence to your spell, saute the carrots with a bit of ginger and butter.

Natalie Zaman

October

Days that turn on a breath into rapidly waning light. Wispy, high dark clouds in an orange and turquoise sky. Bright orange pumpkins carved into beautiful art and lit from inside. The eerie music of screeching cats. These fond images of October burn at a Witch's heart, calling to her even across the seasons where she's busy setting up her tent for festival. By the time October finally arrives, Witches and other magic users have already had discussions about costumes and parties, rituals and celebrations, and we look forward with happiness to the whole month of both poignantly somber and brightly playful activities.

In Celtic Europe, our ancestors acknowledged October as the last month of the summer season, with winter officially beginning on Samhain. They carved slits in squashes to keep light in the fields so they could finish their day's work, and when the custom came to America, it eventually evolved into the tradition of carving jack-o'-lanterns. American Witches often use magical symbols to carve their pumpkins, creating beacons for their Beloved Dead. In the spirit of the turn of energies at this time, we give candy to children to ensure that they, our future, will remember the sweetness inside and be good leaders when their turn comes. May we all be so blessed.

Thuri Calafia

October 1
Monday

3rd ♊

☽ → ♋ 2:00 pm

Color of the day: White
Incense of the day: Rosemary

Open to Receive

Too often we overwork, over-function, and take care of everyone around us. If we rely on accomplishment and productivity to demonstrate our worth, insecurity can turn us into human "doings" instead of human "beings." But each of us was born worthy. Worthy of safety, security, nurture, and love. Worthy of joy, happiness, and success.

Today, release the need to do everything, and be open to receive. Let your kids make you a cup of tea. Receive and feel their love. Let your partner hold you and kiss your head. Receive and feel blessed. Let your cat weave through your legs. Receive and feel wanted. As you go through the day, let people do small things for you (open doors) and give to you (cookies offered at break time). Most of all, create the opening to allow others in. Let them care for you. Stop doing and just be. Open and receive.

Dallas Jennifer Cobb

October 2
Tuesday

3rd ♋

4th Quarter 5:45 am

Color of the day: Scarlet
Incense of the day: Basil

Feast of the Holy Guardian Angels

For centuries, Catholics have honored their guardian angels on this day with prayers and offerings. But whether or not you're Catholic, you have attendant spirit beings that watch over and protect you. Today, create an offering of thanks to them with a white candle, a stick of sweetgrass or copal incense, and one or more white flowers in water. Say:

Spirits of sweetness, spirits of light, those who watch over me all day and night: I offer this candle and this scent of power, with thanks for your presence each minute and hour.

Let the incense burn all the way down. You can let the candle burn all the way down as well, or extinguish and relight it as necessary for safety purposes. Remember to ask your guardian spirits for help regularly, because they are meticulously respectful of our free will and often must wait until their help is invoked.

Tess Whitehurst

October 3
Wednesday

4th ♋

☽ v/c 4:33 am

☽ → ♌ 5:12 pm

Color of the day: Topaz
Incense of the day: Marjoram

Colors, Lights, and Magics

At this time of year, stores begin to fill their shelves with lights for the winter holiday season. With a little foresight, you can stock up on colored lights that will support and boost your spells and craft work.

For example, lights of red, blue, green, or yellow are excellent for elemental magic.

Green is the ideal color for spells seeking money or bounty.

Blue works for meditation, calming, and protection, while yellow works to boost energy.

Silvery-white lights support divination, meditation, and inspiration.

Dark purple and dark blue are useful for binding or banishing work.

Let your own insights and practices help you match colors to your needs. String up the lights in your sanctum sanctorum and plug them in when you want to work with specific intentions. Meditate on the lights' energies and the way they inspire you.

Susan Pesznecker

October 4
Thursday

4th ♌

Color of the day: Green
Incense of the day: Clove

Get Rid of an Unwanted Guest

Try this spell if you have company who has turned from being a guest into a pest. All you need is a broom (magical or everyday), some salt, and a few dried black tea leaves.

If your guest has overstayed their welcome, try to slip out of the room for a moment. Grab your broom and rub the handle vigorously from bottom to top. Say these words quietly or think them:

Broom, broom, without harm,

Help me with this magical charm.

With perfect timing and perfect speed,

Let my guest take their leave!

If possible, lean the broom so the handle is pointing in the direction of your guest. Return to your guest. They will probably seem uncomfortable and will leave soon. After they leave, sprinkle some salt and a few dried tea leaves in the doorway they used as they left. This should get rid of any negativity that may linger.

James Kambos

October 5
Friday

4th ♌

☽ v/c 7:34 am

☽ → ♍ 7:19 pm

Color of the day: Coral
Incense of the day: Yarrow

Divination Enhancement Spell

This October Crone's Sickle moon is the perfect time for early dark time divinations. Make this powder to enhance your divination tools by adding a good pinch each of lavender, cinnamon, rose, and patchouli to a clear glass bowl. Crush and mix the herbs while picturing the Dark Goddess watching over you, approving of your actions and guiding your hands. Say:

Spirit of lavender, easer of hearts, give me compassion in speaking my words.

Spirit of cinnamon, spiritual warrior, give me the drive to stay the path.

Spirit of rose, psychic enhancer, give me the courage to see with clear sight.

Spirit of patchouli, earthy grounder, give me the strength to stand upright.

Keep chanting and crushing the herbs as small as you like. You can even put the herbs in a clean coffee grinder. Sprinkle a little of this powder over your divination tools while speaking the chant three times.

Thuri Calafia

 ## October 6
Saturday

4th ♍

Color of the day: Blue
Incense of the day: Pine

Housecleaning

Saturday is always a good day to clean house. Sometimes our stuff gets hidden away in cabinets and drawers and just lurks there. It's time to clear out all that old stuff.

Start by singing your favorite Goddess chant. As you sing, open every door and drawer in your home. If you find stuff you no longer need, take it out and put it in a bag to donate to an agency that serves people in need.

Now go back to the first open drawer or door and light either a black candle or a smudge stick. As you sing, stop at every open drawer and door and use a feather to direct the clearing energy of the candle or smudge into the space. Finish by standing in the center of your home and sending the energy in the four directions, up and down, and into your heart. Sing as long as you want to.

Barbara Ardinger

October 7
Sunday

4ᵗʰ ♍

☽ v/c 10:03 am

☽ → ♎ 9:10 pm

Color of the day: Yellow
Incense of the day: Marigold

Apple Doll Blessing

Autumn is a great time to enjoy late-season fruits and vegetables, such as pumpkins, apples, figs, cabbages, and kale. Take advantage of these tasty and healthful foods at their peak. Something our family likes to do with extra apples is to create apple dolls as a symbol of abundance and protection.

Peel an apple and carve out facial features. Place the apple on a dowel and let it dry for several weeks. Attach wire for the body, and use fabric scraps to clothe it. Use seeds or buttons for the eyes and yarn for the hair. Place your apple doll near the hearth and say:

Bless this house with
abundance to share,

And protect this home
from winter's glare.

With the power of three times three,

As I will it, so mote it be.

When spring returns, add your apple head to the compost, releasing the spell.

Monica Crosson

October 8
Monday

4ᵗʰ ♎

New Moon 11:47 pm

Color of the day: Ivory
Incense of the day: Neroli

Columbus Day –
Indigenous Peoples' Day

New Moon Pumpkin Picking

Pumpkins are linked to the power of the moon and are aligned with the energies of prosperity and healing. Since it's prime pumpkin season and also a new moon, it's a great time to find the perfect pumpkin to empower with a magical intention. You can keep it until Halloween and then carve it to release the magic.

When you find your ideal pumpkin (one that just feels right and seems to align with your goal), buy it and take it home. Once home, hold the pumpkin and focus strongly on your magical intention (either prosperity or healing) and envision that you are pouring this power into its flesh, where it will stay until you release it.

To release the magic on Halloween, carve the pumpkin with a symbolic face or pattern that represents your goal. Lighting a candle within the completed jack-o'-lantern will set the power free.

Michael Furie

October 9
Tuesday

1st ♎

☽ v/c 4:50 am

Color of the day: Gray
Incense of the day: Bayberry

Spell to See Nature Spirits

This day is the old Greek festival of Gaia and the nymphs. These nature spirits are both male and female entities and are known to be beautiful, sensual, and mischievous. Their descriptions from ancient literature inform our modern-day conception of fairies and other beings.

Early autumn is an evocative time, one that often prompts feelings of nostalgia or moments of déjà vu, suggesting that the veil between the worlds is thinning as we approach the Samhain cross quarter.

Find a quiet spot surrounded by nature (a woodland or meadow is ideal) and sit comfortably. Bring a small offering for the spirits and leave it by a tree or stone. Celtic lore says they love fresh dairy products, but you can also leave fruit, candy, or shiny coins. Try not to make sudden movements or noise. Soon you may notice fleeting movements in your peripheral vision or faint sounds like whispering voices or bells. These may be nature beings trying to communicate with you. What are they trying to say?

Peg Aloi

October 10
Wednesday

1st ♎

☽ → ♏ 12:09 am

Color of the day: White
Incense of the day: Lilac

Good Cents Success Mojo

I love spell bags. These compact bundles of magick can really pack a punch! Because today is the tenth day of the month, it is a good opportunity to harness the qualities of the number's numerological vibration along with the qualities of success and attainment.

Bring to mind a goal you are working toward, and gather a small square of cloth, some ribbon or twine, a small pinch of cinquefoil (five-finger grass), and ten dimes. The dimes pack a triple dose of success energy: you will use ten of them, each dime is worth ten cents, and they are currency.

Place the dimes in a stack on top of the fabric, and sprinkle the cinquefoil over them. Place your hands over the pile, palms down, and focus on your intent, channeling energy into the mojo. Tie up the corners of the fabric with the ribbon or twine, and carry the spell bag in your pocket or place it on your altar.

Blake Octavian Blair

October 11

Thursday

1st ♏

☽ v/c 7:12 pm

Color of the day: Crimson
Incense of the day: Jasmine

healing Wine

The Meditrinalia festival was celebrated by the Romans on this day in honor of Meditrina, a goddess of wine and health. During this time of the waxing moon, you could petition Meditrina if you or a loved one is in need of healing.

Set up a small area to work in and create sacred space within it. Create an offering to Meditrina by crushing grapes and adding herbs to it that aid in healing. As you pour the libation onto the earth, say:

*Meditrina, take this offering made
from the vine to create a healing wine.*

Charlynn Walls

 October 12

Friday

1st ♏

☽ → ♐ 5:53 am

Color of the day: Rose
Incense of the day: Violet

Inspirational Incense

If you're ever feeling a bit stuck in a creative block, grab a stick of your favorite incense and head outdoors. Light the tip and, when you blow out the flame, focus on the element of air within you (the breath) and all around you (the breeze).

Focus intently on the rising smoke while you ask for inspirational energy by saying this rhyme:

*Great and spritely air spirits
who swiftly wax and wane,
release my mental blockages so
creativity may flow again!*

Offer the incense to the spirits of air and to your own spirit guides and guardians.

Repeat the rhyme in your mind or out loud a number of times. Take the incense inside and situate it in the location where you're most creative. As it burns, visualize yourself jumping through a brick wall with the word "blockage" scrawled on it with spray paint. See yourself jumping safely through, shattering the wall and glowing with reinvigorated creativity.

Raven Digitalis

October 13
Saturday

1st ♐

☽ v/c 8:58 pm

Color of the day: Gray
Incense of the day: Rue

The Writing in the Web

This is often a time of year when spiders start to come out of their hiding places, either seeking shelter from the approaching weather in the north or busying themselves for the warmer weather in the Southern Hemisphere. The spider is a very magical creature with much to tell us. Some stories say that the very first language was written in the spider's web. It's the bringer of destiny, the weaver of fate.

Working with spider energy enhances your creativity. If you're planning on participating in November's write-a-thon or starting to make gifts for Yule or Christmas, then invite spider to come and help you by wearing spider-themed jewelry or putting a picture of a spider on your altar or screen saver. If you start to see physical spiders, know that they're coming to help and inspire you as you weave your own web of destiny toward achieving your dreams.

Charlie Rainbow Wolf

October 14
Sunday

1st ♐

☽ → ♑ 3:17 pm

Color of the day: Amber
Incense of the day: Frankincense

Rise from Darkness

Physical exercise can enhance magic; movement activates intention and meditation. When you're feeling low (an affliction all of us deal with many times throughout the course of our lives), try this movement-based meditation to rise from darkness. All you need is a chair.

Begin seated. Feel your feelings; ground yourself in them. Next, visualize a light above your head. Stand up and into the light, and let it flood through you—then sit down again. Try to do this ten times. This exercise, a simple "sit-stand," activates your leg and core muscles and increases circulation. The up-down movement is rhythmic and meditative, but most importantly you are in control, choosing when to rise and when to sit down again. The light is always there.

Enhance this mini magical workout by placing on your temples a drop or two of uplifting oil, such as ylang-ylang, lemon balm, or neroli.

Natalie Zaman

October 15

Monday

1st ♑

Color of the day: Lavender
Incense of the day: Hyssop

Spirit Connection

If you can, do this outside after dusk, or at night in a dimly lit room. Light either a dragon's blood or frankincense incense stick and waft it in the air. Enjoy the scent for a moment and allow it to wash over you. Sit in a comfortable position and close your eyes. Chant:

> *I am one with the spirit,*
> *and the spirit is within me.*

Continue this chant over and over, and feel your power grow. When you feel it is at its height, release the power into the universe. You may want to throw your hands in the air and yell *release!* when you are ready to direct the power into the universe.

Take a moment now to relax. Prepare a pillow and blanket ahead of time, and take a moment to lie down in peace. Focus your attention on receiving any messages Spirit may have for you.

Kerri Connor

October 16
Tuesday

1st ♑

2nd Quarter 2:02 pm

☽ v/c 5:49 pm

Color of the day: Maroon
Incense of the day: Geranium

Blessing for Those Who Protect Us

Hardly a day goes by that we don't hear sirens: police racing to stop a crime or help victimized people, firefighters racing to put out fires in homes and businesses, EMTs racing to rescue and treat injured people. It's important to bless the rescuers and those being rescued.

Whenever you hear a siren, stop what you're doing. Take a deep breath and center and ground yourself. Know that if you were in need, those sirens might be heading in your direction. Say these words:

Blessings for speed and safety to those who are going to help someone.

Blessings for healing and safety to those who are waiting for help.

Blessings to all on the roads and to their destinations.

Or shorten it:

Blessings to you and where you are going.

Take another deep breath, and blow the grounding energy to follow the sirens.

Barbara Ardinger

NOTES:

October 17
Wednesday

2nd ♑

☽ → ♒ 3:36 am

Color of the day: Topaz
Incense of the day: Lavender

Countdown to Samhain (or Any Event!)

Countdown apps are all the rage, but you can go low-tech with a "countdown chain" imbued with spellcraft, correspondences, magical goals, and craft activities. Practice this now with a paper chain designed to prepare you for Samhain.

Choose paper in colors that are appropriate to the date or event. For Samhain, try black, silver, and orange. Cut a 1 x 4-inch strip for each countdown day. On each strip, write a charm, task, affirmation, or instruction. Here are some ideas:

- Pull a tarot card while reflecting on what Samhain will mean to you.

- Create a Samhain incense of sage, cinnamon, cloves, and resin.

- Carve a protective rune into a small pumpkin and leave on the front porch.

- Set up (or tidy up) an ancestor altar.

Staple the strips together, forming a chain, and tack it to the ceiling. Each day, undo a "link" and carry out the action. The chain will be gone on the day of your event, and you'll be ready for it!

Susan Pesznecker

NOTES:

October 18
Thursday

2nd ≈≈

Color of the day: Purple
Incense of the day: Balsam

Media-Free Magic

If "magick is the art of causing changes in consciousness in conformity with the Will," as Dion Fortune says, we can make magnificent change by exercising choice. Use today's energy to augment the power of your will and make enormous changes.

Today, choose to limit your media exposure. Try it for one day. Be mindful of what information you consume. Avoid "junk food" messages and fearmongering. Leave the radio off, bypass the newspaper stand or e-news, and avoid looking at the television, Internet newsfeeds, and Facebook (where so many people repost stories and pictures filled with drama and trauma). Do this just for today.

Tonight, evaluate your energy. Do you feel less anxiety, fear, and dread? Good. Now contemplate extending your choice. The less outside messaging we consume, the more our own true voice will be heard.

Dallas Jennifer Cobb

 October 19
Friday

2nd ≈≈

☽ v/c 8:27 am

☽ → ♓ 4:20 pm

Color of the day: Pink
Incense of the day: Cypress

A Spell to heal a Broken heart

Read the following words to yourself. Follow the instructions to mend a broken heart.

When you've lost that special one,

After a romance is done,

It's time to heal the wound that has scarred your heart.

Even if you think you can't make a fresh start.

It's time to dissolve the grief and bury the past.

You must slowly move forward at last.

Perform this spell after frost has touched the ground,

When summer flowers bow their heads and turn dusty brown.

Go to an orchard when a chill is in the autumn breeze,

Where forgotten apples lay to rot and freeze.

Select an apple that has lost its hue and is pale,

On it, inscribe a heart with a rusty nail.

Crush the apple into the earth so
the spell's power is released.

Walk away, hold your head high,
let your heart be at peace.

James Kambos

NOTES:

October 20
Saturday

2nd ♓

Color of the day: Black
Incense of the day: Patchouli

Scatter to the Winds

This spell is designed to be a quick and gentle means of releasing us from obstacles to success. Obtain as many leaves as desired (three to five is ideal). It helps if the leaves are different colors. Also, have a black bowl to set the leaves in after they're charged.

To begin, think of specific things that you wish to be free of, and charge one leaf for each item. To charge, hold the leaf in your hands and focus on the problem. Send it into the leaf. After the leaf is charged, place it in the black bowl. Once all the leaves have been prepared, take the bowl outside and scatter the leaves to the winds, saying:

*Mother Nature, please take away
these things that no longer serve
me, released from these, the ties
that bind, letting me go free.*

Walk away without looking back and wash the bowl with soap and water.

Michael Furie

October 21

Sunday

2nd ♓

☽ v/c 7:47 pm

Color of the day: Orange
Incense of the day: Almond

Coming of Autumn Spell

The ancient Greek women's festival of Thesmophoria was said to take place during October around this time. The rite lasted several days and was an elaborate and mysterious ritual dedicated to Demeter and the narrative surrounding the abduction and return of her daughter Kore/Persephone (which brought winter to the land). Women dressed in white, spread herbs on their beds, and sat on the ground to help bless the planting of the autumn corn crop (this was meant to symbolize keeping Kore safe in the underworld). Reading or acting out the Demeter/Kore myth is a powerful way to attune yourself to these seasonal energies.

To recreate this rite, wear a white robe and create a sacred space where you can plant some kernels of corn or another grain (either in a container or in the ground). After planting the corn, sit nearby and offer blessings to the earth mother Demeter, asking for her nurturance of and protection for the earth and her daughter Kore (who will be born again in spring's flora).

Peg Aloi

October 22

Monday

2nd ♓

☽ → ♈ 2:58 am

Color of the day: Gray
Incense of the day: Narcissus

Love Your Body Spell

This spell starts with a shower. While cleansing yourself, think about all the things our culture tells you that are currently issues for you. As you wash, tell yourself that you are washing yourself of society's ridiculous notions of what a person's body is supposed to look like and be like. Get angry if you need to: talk it out, shout it out, cry and mourn without shame.

After you dry off, go to your altar, naked, and visualize your chosen deities looking at you with love and approval. Say:

I was made by the gods and goddesses and am therefore perfect just as I am.

Imagine a world where everyone looks just like you and where your body is considered the ideal form of beauty and strength. Allow yourself to Just. Feel. That.

Then light a red candle and focus on your vitality, your vibrance. Open your arms and let the warm red light come into you, filling you with courage and pride in yourself. Be blessed.

Thuri Calafia

October 23
Tuesday

2nd ♈

☉ → ♏ 7:22 am

☽ v/c 2:18 pm

Color of the day: White
Incense of the day: Ylang-ylang

Warrior Witch Bottle

A couple of years ago, a series of nearby home invasions were more than a little alarming. When it comes to my home and family, the gardening gloves come off and the Warrior Witch gets ready to stir up some real protective power. I like to do this by making a Witch bottle. Originally made of clay, Witch bottles were used to ward off attacks by Witches and malicious spirits, but we can use them as a way to protect home and family.

In an old canning jar, place some hair or fingernail clippings from everyone in the family and/or your pets, broken glass, rusty nails and pins, protective herbs, soil from your yard, salt, and rice to absorb negative energy. Seal the lid of the jar with black wax and say:

Absorb all negativity and keep back those who mean harm.

I invoke protection with the words of this charm.

Tuck your Witch bottle away.

Monica Crosson

October 24
Wednesday

2nd ♈

☽ → ♉ 10:33 am

Full Moon 12:45 pm

Color of the day: Yellow
Incense of the day: Marjoram

Call to Athena

On this day of the full moon, you can reach out to Athena for wisdom when implementing any change you desire. Today you can also tap into the energies associated with Wednesday, which can be used for communication and change.

You can petition Athena for assistance by taking a drawing of an owl and coloring it with gold, yellow, green, and blue. Place the completed drawing on your altar, and anoint it with orange or cedar oil. Take a moment to focus your energies on the change you are seeking. Call out to Athena, saying:

Athena, lend your wisdom on this change, so if necessary I can rearrange.

Leave the drawing on the altar until the next full moon.

Charlynn Walls

·October 25
Thursday

3rd ♉

Color of the day: Turquoise
Incense of the day: Myrrh

Blessing of the Animals

We Pagans don't have to wait for one day a year to bless the animals. Do this spell as often as you want to. Bless the creatures who live in our homes, the animals on our farms, and the wild animals in our cities and the wilderness. Remember that we don't "own" any animals, because we cannot own another soul. That's enslavement.

To bless the creatures who share our homes, buy some bird, cat, dog, or reptile treats and stand or kneel beside the animal, cage, terrarium, or aquarium. Give the animal a treat and pet it (if possible) and say:

The Goddess blesses you and
loves you. I honor you and
share my home with you.

For feral or wild animals (cats, squirrels, pigeons, crows, etc.), set out a few treats and speak the same words. For creatures like coyotes, bears, and alligators for whom it's not safe in your neighborhood, throw the treats into their territory and speak only the first sentence of the blessing.

Barbara Ardinger

·October 26
Friday

3rd ♉

☽ v/c 10:49 am

☽ → ♊ 3:41 pm

Color of the day: Purple
Incense of the day: Rose

Apple Self-Acceptance Meditation

Friday's planetary ruler is Venus. Venus of course is known for its resonance with love energy and magick. Apples are also ruled by Venus and are quite a seasonal favorite. Love is more than romantic love; it is the love that is self-acceptance as well.

Today, find an apple. Make the choosing process part of the magick. Find one that you find beautiful, realizing that imperfections do not dilute beauty. Once you have found an apple you resonate with, put it on your altar and meditate while gazing upon it. Notice that even with imperfections, it has its own beauty, without and within. Its appearance, how it was created, and everything about it is simply magickal and beautiful. Look closely at it. Notice that even where it looks perfect there are imperfections, perhaps perfect imperfections. Know that you, even if imperfect, are beautiful just like the apple.

Blake Octavian Blair

October 27

Saturday

3rd ♊

Color of the day: Indigo
Incense of the day: Sage

Balancing Your Thought Processes

The days leading up to Samhain are ideal for banishing and balancing. Because magick is guided so heavily by our thought processes, it's essential to keep ourselves in check at all times. The path of mystical consciousness is, by nature, the path of self-improvement.

We are all prone to insecurity, doubt, and a pessimistic outlook rooted in our younger years. Regardless of your age, try this simple everyday magick for rerouting your mental processes.

Place a small black stone (such as obsidian) in your left pocket, and place a white stone (such as quartz) in your right pocket. When you catch yourself thinking bitter, destructive, insecure, or otherwise negative thoughts rooted in old patterns, grip the black stone and focus the energies into the piece. Next, while touching or holding the white stone, replace the thoughts with positive, balanced, uplifting, and hopeful thoughts while drawing energy from the stone. Continue this as long

as you'd like, then conclude by tossing the black stone in running water and keeping the white stone on your altar.

Raven Digitalis

NOTES:

October 28

Sunday

3rd ♊

☽ v/c 12:37 am

☽ → ♋ 7:27 pm

Color of the day: Gold

Incense of the day: Hyacinth

Boundary Lines

Today in 1767 the Mason-Dixon line was established, creating a boundary that later divided the North and South in the American Civil War. Have you ever felt that you needed to set a defined boundary between you and someone with whom you had little in common? To do this, you'll need a short stick and two stones of contrasting colors. Black and white work best, but any other combination will do.

Place the stick on a windowsill or shelf, and put one stone on either side of it. Every day move the stones a little bit farther apart from each other, and as you do so, say:

You don't see it, but I am gone.

Little by little, make a conscious effort to cease your activities and communication with the other person. Be polite but not encouraging. You'll soon drift apart, usually without any huge confrontation.

Charlie Rainbow Wolf

October 29

Monday

3rd ♋

Color of the day: White

Incense of the day: Clary sage

National Cat Day

Cat lovers, rejoice: it's National Cat Day! Today, bless your own cat(s) and/or the cats of the world with the following spell.

Assemble a simple altar with a statue or image of the cat goddess Bast and a clear quartz crystal. If you have cats, add an image of each one. Anoint the Bast image and the image of your cat(s) with essential oil of myrrh. Say:

Cats close to home and cats of the earth, I honor your presence, I honor your worth. As you bless our planet with beauty and grace, may all cats be healthy and happily placed.

If you have a cat or cats, spend some quality time with them. Maybe play with them, pet or brush them, offer them some catnip, or give them a treat. Also consider making a donation to a local cat shelter or even fostering cats or kittens who need a home.

Tess Whitehurst

·October 30

Tuesday

3rd ♋

☽ v/c 10:31 pm

☽ → ♌ 10:42 pm

Color of the day: Red

Incense of the day: Cedar

Samhain Protection Cider

U se your kitchen witchery skills to whip up this lovely hot drink to protect you through the Samhain season. You will need:

- 1 gallon apple cider
- 3 cloves
- 1 tablespoon cinnamon
- 1 teaspoon ginger
- 1 teaspoon nutmeg
- 4 slices of lemon

Pour the cider into a pot on the stove (or into a slow cooker). Add the spices one by one, stirring constantly as you do. Focus your intention or protection into the cider. As you add each item, say:

Bless this (name of ingredient).

Protect my family and myself.

After the spices are all added, lay the lemon slices on top (say the same phrase) and allow the cider to simmer for ten minutes. Pour a cup for everyone and envision protection as you sip away at this tasty treat.

Kerri Connor

·October 31
Wednesday

3rd ♌

4th Quarter 12:40 pm

Color of the day: Brown
Incense of the day: Honeysuckle

Samhain – halloween

Pumpkin Ancestor Altar

Samhain is a time for remembering and honoring our loved ones who have passed. Create an ancestor altar using Halloween's favorite fruit: pumpkins.

Cut your pumpkin as if you were making a jack-o'-lantern. Scoop out the seeds, then wash and dry them. Instead of creating a face on the pumpkin, carve your ancestors' names or initials into the flesh, speaking them aloud as you work. You can also paint the names or initials on the pumpkin. If you go this route, drill small holes into the pumpkin so that it still acts as a lantern.

Dry out the pumpkin as best you can, then put the seeds back in with this blessing:

Dearly departed

But always present,

Bless what's inside

With your presence.

Place a tealight on top of the seeds and put the pumpkin outside to light up the night until the candle goes out.

The next day, take out the seeds and save them to plant next year.

Natalie Zaman

NOTES:

November

The sounds of nature begin to quiet down in November, but this month is far from silent. Yes, the cheery morning birdsong of spring is gone, and crickets are no longer fiddling on warm summer afternoons, but November has its own "voices." On a frosty November morning, you'll hear a faint, faraway gabble. Raise your eyes toward the sky, and coming over the horizon, in a V formation heading south, is a flock of wild geese. The sound makes you pause and wonder: how do they know it's time to migrate? As you rake leaves, the late autumn breeze stirs them, and they softly rustle as they click and swirl up the street. Few sounds say November like the wind. It may be as gentle as a baby's breath or it may roar, carrying the weight of the coming winter as it howls in the night. During the night you can also hear November's most haunting voice: the lone hooting of an owl. Yes, this month has many voices, but every evening I hear the most comforting voice of all. That voice belongs to the crackling of burning logs as my hearth fire wards off the chill of a dark November night.

During this mysterious month, let the voices of November speak to you, igniting your imagination and your magic.

James Kambos

November 1
Thursday

4th ♌

Color of the day: White
Incense of the day: Carnation

All Saints' Day

Past Life Spell

Sometimes our past-life baggage can trip us up and cause problems in our current life. Often, healing these energy patterns can become our life's purpose.

For this spell, inscribe one black candle for your patron god and one for your matron goddess. Cast your circle and call the quarters in your usual way, and then say:

> *I am here to learn about the energies from my past lives that still need healing. I am open to learning about who and what I was. Please, Lord and Lady, give clarity to my meditation.*

Make yourself comfortable and visualize your spirit backing out of your body and drifting backward until you find yourself in another body—your body in a past life that has significance to the life you're living today. Stay open to the lessons your gods present for you to learn, and allow time and space for the meditation.

Once you've risen from the work, jot down any relevant things you saw or heard. Going forward, work to heal those energies.

Thuri Calafia

November 2
Friday

4th ♌

☽ v/c 12:32 am

☽ → ♍ 1:48 am

Color of the day: Rose
Incense of the day: Alder

All Souls Day Cemetery Visit

Today the celebrations of our beloved dead continue! Today is All Souls Day in Catholic traditions, and the day also holds celebrations of the Mexican Dia de los Muertos! I invite you to join me in a favorite activity of mine for this day: cemetery visits. Many traditional celebrations involve honoring your own relatives, and you certainly may visit their graves if they are nearby; however, many of us do not live near the graves of our relatives. In this case, visiting local cemeteries still honors the spirits of those who came before you where you live, ancestors of the land, if you will.

I like to stroll the graveyard, clean off any obscured stones or toppled decorations, and leave offerings about the grounds, especially at the gates. Tobacco, apples, and corn make nice offerings. Honoring those different from you also shows respect for diversity to those beyond the veil.

Blake Octavian Blair

November 3

Saturday

4th ♏

Color of the day: Brown

Incense of the day: Magnolia

Shoe Sachet for Safe Travels

It's holiday time—which means traveling, be it journeys to visit family, shopping trips, or just being outdoors and enjoying the sights and sounds and scents of the season. With so many people out and about, a travel talisman is in order. Back when folks traveled mainly on foot, it was customary to pop a few herbs into one's boots to ensure a safe journey.

Make a sachet to slip into your shoes (when you're not wearing them) to freshen them up and charge them with travel-friendly energy. Mix together equal amounts of mugwort (to prevent weariness), comfrey (for safety and protection), and mint (refreshing and hospitable), with this incantation:

Near and far,

By foot or car,

Keep me safe where I go.

I will it be so!

Place the mixture in black (protective) pouches and tuck them into your shoes—just remember to take them out before wearing!

Natalie Zaman

November 4

Sunday

4th ♏

☽ v/c 2:26 am

☽ → ♎ 4:01 am

Color of the day: Amber

Incense of the day: Juniper

Daylight Saving Time

ends at 2:00 a.m.

Reenergize Yourself

When daylight saving time ends, we gain an extra hour. This is a great time to recharge yourself and regain energy during the dark part of the year.

If you are able to go outside, you may want to sit directly on the ground. However, if you cannot, you could bring some earth into your home in an altar bowl. Create sacred space around the area you are working in. Touch the earth and connect with the energies within it. Draw those energies into you as you take a deep breath. Continue until you feel fully energized, as doing so will help you through the rest of the year.

Charlynn Walls

November 5

Monday

4th ♎

Color of the day: Silver
Incense of the day: Neroli

Bonfire Night

On Guy Fawkes Day, people celebrate the famous English rebel who sought to overthrow a corrupt government, and recite this rhyme: "Remember, remember, the fifth of November!" The event is still commemorated every year with bonfires, which creates a dynamic social opportunity for people to gather outside in autumn.

You can create your own bonfire and use it to magically transform your intentions. Build a small fire outside in a fire pit or fire dish or inside in a flameproof cauldron. Participants should write down something they wish to transform in their lives, imbue it with their will and intention, then fold the paper and throw it into the flames.

Peg Aloi

 November 6

Tuesday

4th ♎

☽ v/c 3:19 am
☽ → ♏ 8:02 am

Color of the day: Black
Incense of the day: Ginger

Election Day (general)

Bury a Curse Spell

If you think you've been cursed, try this spell. If possible, perform this spell on a rainy day. Write the nature of the curse on paper. Describe what kind of curse you think it is, and why you feel you've been cursed. Take the paper and a shovel or hoe to a secluded area. Begin to dig a "grave" for your curse as you say:

> *Curse, hear the power of this charm.*
>
> *In this grave you'll dissolve into harmless dust,*
>
> *And no longer will you cause me harm.*
>
> *Father Sky, drench this grave with a cleansing shower.*
>
> *Mother Earth, destroy this curse's power.*

Drop the paper into the grave. Pack the loose soil over the paper using the shovel or hoe. Walk away, knowing the powers of Father Sky and Mother Earth are cleansing and destroying the curse. As the paper decays and the writing fades, the curse's power will weaken.

James Kambos

NOTES:

 November 7
Wednesday

4th ♏

New Moon 11:02 am

Color of the day: Yellow
Incense of the day: Bay laurel

Uncover Your hidden Desires

Here is a fun variation on the old standby of setting an intention at the new moon. Ideally, do this after dark by a natural body of water. Otherwise, a fountain, a pond, or even a cauldron of water will do.

Hold a pyrite in your right hand and charge it with the intention to reach deep into your soul and reclaim some of its hidden depths. Then throw or place the stone in the water. Now fearlessly dive into your hidden desires. What do you really want: in your career, your finances, your relationships? Go beyond what you have assumed you wanted or what you used to want. Write down what you discover.

On a fresh page, phrase your newly uncovered desires in the present tense, as if they are already true. At the bottom of the page, write:

Thank you, universe, for this or something even better!

Then sign and date.

Tess Whitehurst

November 8
Thursday

1st ♏

☽ v/c 5:42 am

☽ → ♐ 1:59 pm

Color of the day: Green
Incense of the day: Apricot

Now I Lay Me Down to Sleep

We're a week past Samhain, the year's final harvest. The nights are longer and bedtime is very attractive.

Speak this nighttime blessing tonight—and all through the winter. As you say it, think about the blessings of the Pagan religion and the Pagan lifestyle, with its regular rituals and interesting mythologies. We don't pray to a god who will take our soul in the night. We pray to goddesses and gods (and possibly elementals and fairies and who knows who else—we're an independent bunch) who touch our lives with caring and tenderness while they also sometimes hand us challenges. We are highly fortunate folks.

Now I lay me down to sleep,

Blessed Goddess, in your keep,

Send sweet dreams the whole night through

And keep me faithful, good, and true.

And in the morn, when I awake,

Gentle Goddess, feed me cake!

Barbara Ardinger

Notes:

November 9
Friday

1st ♐

Color of the day: Purple
Incense of the day: Vanilla

Success Prep

This spell is designed to help you achieve success in whatever it is you are working on. It can be success in a relationship, at school, at work, or even in a court case.

Take a piece of green paper and write down on it what you are working on that you want to be successful in. Be as specific as possible. Write down also what you are doing in the mundane world to help ensure this success. Roll the paper up into a scroll and bind it with black ribbon three times. As you bind it, say:

I bind this scroll once, twice, thrice,
binding success to me in my endeavor.

Bury the scroll either in your yard or at a crossroads. If you can't access either of those, you can hide the scroll in the dirt of a potted plant.

Kerri Connor

November 10
Saturday

1st ♐

☽ v/c 10:35 pm
☽ → ♑ 10:55 pm

Color of the day: Blue
Incense of the day: Ivy

Random Acts of Magic

You've heard of Random Acts of Kindness Day. Why not make today Random Acts of Magic Day? Use your imagination and dream up ways to perform small acts of magic for friends, family, and strangers. Radiate magic, and send your witchy vibes out to work their magic.

Find opportunities to conduct magic throughout the day by blessing strangers, granting wishes to your kids, creating a ritual with your family members, writing simple spells for friends, and leaving blessings for neighbors. Your magical acts can be obviously Pagan or covertly magical. Take cookies to your coworkers or invite a friend out for "cakes and ale." Quietly bless and protect your office, or place a pentagram over the door.

Spread your magic around, touching people and transforming them in positive ways. These small acts of magic can consciously change your own and other people's energy, and can create positive associations with *Pagans* and *magic*.

Dallas Jennifer Cobb

November 11
Sunday

1st ♑

Color of the day: Orange
Incense of the day: Heliotrope

Veterans Day

Lest We Forget

The first Remembrance Day was on this day in 1919 to commemorate the agreement ending the First World War, on the eleventh hour of the eleventh day in the eleventh month. Eleven is a very special number. In numerology it's considered a master number. It's thought to be the most intuitive of all the numbers and to have a special connection to the unconscious.

The number eleven invites your spirit to grow. As you pause to remember the fallen, the veterans, or even just to contemplate what it would be like if there were an end to all wars, open yourself to the vibration that eleven brings. Quiet your mind and let the peace that passes all understanding fill your soul. Whether you call this day Remembrance Day, Armistice Day, or Veterans Day, keep in mind those who have served, wish them peace, and remember the price they paid for it.

Charlie Rainbow Wolf

November 12
Monday

1st ♑

Color of the day: Ivory
Incense of the day: Lily

Smashing Pumpkins for Further Protection

Jack-o'-lanterns represent protection from harmful forces. Their scary and funny faces have long served to distract negative spirits and keep them at bay from one's property.

In many parts of the Western world, people leave jack-o'-lanterns on their porch throughout November, until the Halloween decor is replaced with Yuletide charm. If you are one of these people, take your pumpkins to the edge of your property and smash them while saying this:

Harmful forces, now be gone!
Only protection can carry on!

Leave the pieces of the pumpkin around your property so they can continue protecting the land.

If you have a friend or family member who gives you permission to do the same on their own property, go for it! Just don't go around smashing pumpkins around the neighborhood without prior approval.

For an additional boost, do this magick while playing some music from my all-time favorite band, the Smashing Pumpkins!

Raven Digitalis

November 13

Tuesday

1st ♑

☽ v/c 10:13 am

☽ → ♒ 10:45 am

Color of the day: Maroon

Incense of the day: Basil

A Potion for Passion

Long, dark evenings make November a great time to rekindle the flame of love. Stir up a little romance for you and your partner with this sweet concoction:

Cinnamon-Spiked Hot Chocolate

2 cups half and half

2 teaspoons honey

½ teaspoon espresso powder

8 ounces grated dark chocolate (70%)

2 cinnamon sticks

Whipped cream

Heat the first four ingredients in a saucepan at a medium to low temperature until small bubbles form. Pour into mugs. Add a cinnamon stick to each and top with whipped cream.

Anoint two red candles with cinnamon oil and set on a low table somewhere cozy with the hot chocolate.

Invoke the candles and chocolate with your intent by saying:

Love is in the air this
dark winter's night.

May the flame of our passion
burn hot and bright!

Enjoy!

Monica Crosson

Notes:

November 14
Wednesday

1st ♒

Color of the day: White
Incense of the day: Lavender

Photo Feet for the Travel Season

In a simple act of sympathetic magic, many Witches scoop up dirt from their footprints (in their yard, driveway, etc.), keeping it with them to help them travel safely and find their way back home. In my home of Portland, Oregon, people have likewise adopted the custom of taking photographs of their feet standing on the airport carpet, ready to leave on an adventure. Subconsciously they're enacting a similar wish for safe travel and a safe return home.

As you leave your home and prepare to travel, take a smartphone photo of your feet, either at home or at your travel jump-off point. Looking at your feet, repeat:

Travel is fun, but home is sweet;
Fleet may be my photo feet.

Gaze at the photo as needed throughout your trip, anchoring your connection with your home. When it's time to return, look again at the photo, saying:

There's no place like home.

Susan Pesznecker

 ## November 15
Thursday

1st ♒

2nd Quarter 9:54 am

☾ v/c 10:58 pm

☾ → ♓ 11:41 pm

Color of the day: Turquoise
Incense of the day: Jasmine

Spell to Become Your Own Best Friend

For this spell, you will need a pillar candle in your favorite color and a taper candle in a healing color (it's okay if they're the same color). Take some time to decide what it is that you have to offer a friendship and what you most need from a friendship. Chances are they're the same, or very similar, and are along the lines of nurturing.

Carve the pillar with symbols of your strongest needs (for example, a dollar sign for money or a heart for love or physical health). Then take the taper and light it, letting some melted wax form. Hold the healing taper candle over the pillar, and let the healing-color wax fill in the "holes" in your spirit. Say:

As the moon grows, let my light
and my love for myself grow.
I AM my own best friend.

Follow up by gifting yourself with a favorite cookie and drink for cakes and wine, followed by a "date"—a favorite dinner and movie perhaps. Focus on treating yourself like a best friend and let the magic happen!

Thuri Calafia

NOTES:

 November 16

Friday

2nd ♓

Color of the day: Rose
Incense of the day: Thyme

Spell for Abundance

Just before winter arrives is a good time to make plans to increase prosperity. It's also a good time to think about our needs versus our wants and to clarify what abundance means for us. For this spell, gather three personal items: one you absolutely need, one you like but don't need, and one that is not necessary at all. Place the items in front of you. Pick up the first one and say:

I am blessed to have all that I need.

Put it down, then pick up the second item and say:

I am capable of working
for the things I desire.

Put down the second item and pick up the third, saying:

I can let go of what does not serve me.

Look at all three items and say:

I have an abundance of riches in my life.

Give the third item to charity or a friend. Do this spell once a month to help you purge your unnecessary belongings, to reinforce your positive efforts to build prosperity, and to remind you of what you need and want in your life.

Peg Aloi

November 17
Saturday

2nd ♓

Color of the day: Indigo
Incense of the day: Sandalwood

Gifting to Others

Today is Use Less Stuff Day. On this day, we are challenged to create less waste and be more cognizant of conservation of natural resources.

Take a moment to look at what you use on a regular basis and what you do not, especially in regard to your altar and magickal practice. If there is something you haven't utilized in the last six months, consider passing it on to someone who can use it. If you don't know anyone who might be able to make use of it, consider passing it on to an organization that could raffle it off or redistribute it as part of their outreach program. Not only are you cleaning up your own clutter, which will help your energy flow in a more efficient manner, but you are also helping someone else out in the process!

Charlynn Walls

November 18
Sunday

2nd ♓

☽ v/c 3:04 am
☽ → ♈ 10:56 am

Color of the day: Gold
Incense of the day: Eucalyptus

Carry On

What is November good for? Except for Thanksgiving, it's an often dreary month without a sabbat. About all we can think about is being lazy, maybe reading a juicy novel or two, and taking naps. But we always have work to do. Sing this marching song and get back to work:

When all the world is gloom and gray—carry on.

When nature everywhere's asleep—carry on.

We know there's always work to do—carry on.

Great magic calls us every day—carry on.

When all I want to do is sleep—carry on.

I know Great Work still beckons me—carry on.

And I shall take the unknown road—carry on.

For I have promises to keep—carry on.

You can chant this as a call and
response with your friends.

Barbara Ardinger

Notes:

November 19

Monday

2nd ♈

Color of the day: Gray
Incense of the day: Hyssop

Passion Pot

Scorpio energy is intense—not
unlike Isabella, the heroine
of John Keats's poem "The Pot of
Basil." Isabella keeps her passion alive
by burying the head of her murdered
lover in a pot of basil, a lusty plant.

Draw on Scorpio's brooding intensity and basil's power of passion by
growing a pot of basil for magical
use. Before you plant your basil,
cleanse and charge a piece of rose
quartz (heart-shaped, if possible).
Put some soil in the base of the pot,
then nestle in the rose quartz with
these words:

Basil, sweet, intense in flavor,

Drink deep the love that is my favor.

Seep into root and leaf and stem

For when I need it, now and then.

Isabella watered her basil with tears.
You can as well, but regular or moon-
charged water will do. Incorporate your
basil into recipes and any spells that
call for passion—but use sparingly!

Natalie Zaman

November 20
Tuesday

2nd ♈

☽ v/c 5:46 pm

☽ → ♉ 6:43 pm

Color of the day: Red
Incense of the day: Cinnamon

Dinner with Ebisu

The twentieth day of every month is special to the Japanese god Ebisu. Ebisu is a god of luck, commerce, and good business. Businesspeople hold lavish luncheons featuring a large altar to Ebisu. Upon entering the luncheon, each attendee places an offering on the altar before an image of Ebisu.

Ebisu also attempts to ensure that people act fairly in business deals. We ourselves may not be able to hold this ceremonial lunch at our place of employment. However, we can honor the gods of business at dinnertime in our homes in an adaptation of this celebration.

Erect an altar to the business gods, and include an image of Ebisu to honor his inspiration. Have each member of the household place an offering upon the table, along with something from their field of employment, perhaps their business card or a related tool or implement. Ask for the gods' blessings upon your endeavors.

Blake Octavian Blair

November 21
Wednesday

2nd ♉

Color of the day: Brown
Incense of the day: Lilac

Purification Shower Bath

A lot of pre-ritual instructions advise taking a bath to cleanse the body and spirit of any disharmonious energy. Many adults with hectic schedules are not used to taking a bath and only have time for a quick shower. Others don't really care for baths and prefer to shower exclusively. Sometimes a cleansing shower doesn't feel as thorough to me, so I like to combine the two to get the best of both options.

If you run a shower and leave the drain plug in, the bathtub will slowly fill with water. Pour a cup of Epsom salts, a cup of regular salt, and a cup of lemon juice into the tub, and as it fills, you basically create a purification mixture that pulls out any unwanted energies through your legs and feet. Just watch the water level so that you can drain the tub before it overflows.

Michael Furie

November 22

Thursday

2nd ♉

☉ → ♐ 4:01 am

☽ v/c 4:59 am

☽ → ♊ 11:10 pm

Color of the day: Purple
Incense of the day: Nutmeg

Thanksgiving Day

Give Thanks

The American holiday for giving thanks is a powerful day for abundance even if you don't live in the United States. Millions of people are celebrating their thankfulness today, and this power is sent out into the universe. If you don't live in the US, make sure to still spend some time today being thankful for all you have been given.

For those who do live in the US, be sure to leave an offering to your deities for your thankfulness for your abundance. Remind yourself that not everyone has everything they need. Invite someone who doesn't have a place to go to share in your day.

This day also starts the "giving season." Look into opportunities to volunteer or share your abundance with others, but keep in mind that while many charities get help at this time of year, help is needed all year long. Keep the spirit of giving thanks alive throughout the year.

Kerri Connor

 November 23

Friday

2nd ♊

Full Moon 12:39 am

Color of the day: Coral
Incense of the day: Yarrow

Manipulating Time

The very first episode of *Doctor Who* aired in Britain on this day in 1963. We're all time lords in our own way, and even if you're unfamiliar with this TV series, you can prove this to yourself. Ever notice how time seems to speed up when you're enjoying yourself but slow down when you're bored? You can use that phenomenon to stretch and fold time, and you won't need a TARDIS to do it!

If you need to slow time down, just envision the earth slowing as it turns. Of course, this won't actually stop the clock—a minute is a minute is a minute! What it will do is influence the perception of time so that everyone's awareness allows them to get more done in less time. If you need to accelerate time, focus on the earth's rotation speeding up. It sounds oversimplified, but it does work!

Charlie Rainbow Wolf

November 24
Saturday

3rd ♊

Color of the day: Gray
Incense of the day: Rue

Post and Pre-holiday Detox

Whether or not you celebrated Thanksgiving a couple of days ago, today is an excellent day for a detoxifying cleanse. In addition to balancing out any past food-related extravagances, we can also do this with the intention to help us make balanced and healthy choices in the famously decadent month ahead.

As soon as you wake up, light a white candle anointed with essential oil of peppermint. Center yourself and take some deep, cleansing breaths, bringing fresh, invigorating white light into your entire body and your every cell. Throughout the day, drink at least half your body weight in ounces of pure water. Abstain from all sweeteners, refined flours (whole grains are fine), dairy products, alcohol, and coffee (tea is fine). Also go light on the fruit juice, although have as much whole fruit and vegetable juice as you like. And, of course, go big on the vegetables, herbs, spices, beans, and nuts.

Tess Whitehurst

November 25
Sunday

3rd ♊

☽ v/c 12:31 am
☽ → ♋ 1:38 am

Color of the day: Yellow
Incense of the day: Frankincense

Hot Wax Divination

This simple divination technique originated in Eastern Europe. It's easy to use. You'll need a new white candle, some olive oil, and a dark-colored bowl or cauldron filled with water.

First, using a drop of olive oil, "dress" your candle. To do this, rub a bit of olive oil between your hands, then rub the candle. Begin in the center and rub toward the wick. Next, start in the center and rub toward the bottom of the candle. Your candle is ready.

Think of a question you want answered. Light the candle. Tilt the candle so three drops of wax drop into the bowl/cauldron filled with water. Snuff out the candle. When the drops of wax harden, "read" their shapes to answer your question. Interpret them as best you can. You'll get better at it the more you do this. The candle may be used again for magic.

James Kambos

November 26
Monday

3rd ♋

Color of the day: White
Incense of the day: Rosemary

Caught at the Crossroads Spell

There comes a time in our lives when we come to a crossroads. Which road will lead us to a happy, fulfilled life? Should we take the road less traveled or stick to the path that feels safe? Maybe you're a teenager heading off to college—which school is the right one for you? Or maybe a new job opportunity has arisen in another state.

At such a time, call upon Hecate, goddess of wisdom. Decorate your altar with Hecate's symbols, including keys, black dog figures, poppies, and hazelnuts. Light a black candle for the wisdom of the crone and say:

Hecate of wisdom and revealer of insight,

I come to the crossroads on this night.

Illuminate the path that is right for me.

As I will it, so mote it be!

Close your eyes and picture yourself at the crossroads. Let the torch of the crone illuminate the path that is right for you.

Monica Crosson

November 27
Tuesday

3rd ♋

☽ v/c 2:22 am

☽ → ♌ 3:35 am

Color of the day: Scarlet
Incense of the day: Bayberry

Making Friends with Mercury Retrograde

We're right smack in the middle of the final Mercury retrograde of 2018. A friend of mine calls it Mercury "wrecktrograde," as everything seems to go wrong during this period.

Conventional wisdom suggests that we sit tight, avoiding new ventures, projects, or travel during a Mercury retrograde. It also claims that even the best plans can easily go awry during this period and that communication and relationships will be especially challenging. Magic folks may find their spider senses all atingle during this time, feeling edgy and unsettled.

How to stay calm during Mercury retrograde? Try this meditation. Picture yourself on a rollercoaster. Imagine it speeding along the track while you hold on tight. Feel the ups and downs, the twists and turns. Understand that even though the ride is bumpy, your grip is secure. You're safe. See yourself coming to a smooth, flat piece of track. The ride slows and evens out. The craziness stops, and you relax and enjoy the view. Realize that Mercury retrograde, too, will come to a smooth end.

Susan Pesznecker

NOTES:

November 28
Wednesday

3rd ♌

Color of the day: Topaz
Incense of the day: Marjoram

An Empathic Spell for Emotional Boundaries

In 2016 I was lucky enough to publish a book called *Esoteric Empathy*. While performing research, I realized the profound extent to which empathy is growing as a biological and spiritual force. It is quite literally changing the world!

Everyone is empathic to one degree or another. For those of us who are especially emotionally absorptive (sometimes called "empaths"), little spells such as this one can be helpful when we have accidentally taken on too much emotional energy from outside sources. If you feel this way, my quick-spell suggestion is to meditate and calm your mind in a darkened room. Next, surround yourself with a small circle of salt. (For an additional boost, use the herbs yarrow, rue, and black pepper.) Imagine this circle growing into a mighty sphere of crystalline light all around your body.

Once the circle is established, declare the following multiple times aloud and silently until you feel protected:

*Mighty spirits, please come
help me build this sphere! My
emotions are protected and
those of others are cleared!*

Raven Digitalis

NOTES:

November 29

Thursday

3rd ♌

☽ v/c 4:47 am

☽ → ♍ 6:08 am

4th Quarter 7:19 pm

Color of the day: Crimson
Incense of the day: Mulberry

Magical Dishwashing

For most practitioners who align the seasons with the four elements, autumn is linked to the power of water. The energy of water is magnetic in nature and is tied to emotion and intuition. Connecting to water can help to heal and nurture our spiritual and emotional selves.

Though a relaxing candlelit bath with incense and exotic oils can be spiritually cleansing and recharging, our busy lives don't always allow for such luxuries. If quick showers are a way of life, a longer connection to water can be achieved during a mundane activity: washing dishes. Scrubbing a sink full of dishes can be a meditative act if you allow yourself to zone out. Just connect to the power of the water to cleanse and heal. You can will that it pull any incorrect or harmful energies from you, thereby cleansing your dishes and your aura.

Michael Furie

 November 30

Friday

4th ♍

Color of the day: Pink
Incense of the day: Mint

Absorbing Negativity

With the days growing shorter and the nights growing longer, it's easy to slip into a bit of a funk at this time of year. Time to do a little SAD first aid. SAD, or seasonal affective disorder, is a mild depression that happens as a result of the lessened levels of sunlight and the resultant lower levels of vitamin D produced within the human body.

Meditate this morning, sitting quietly for ten minutes before your day starts. Close your eyes. Breathe in, pause, then exhale. Envision yourself surrounded by white light. Breathe the light into your chest. Pause and feel it travel into your head. Exhale it out the top of your head and cascade it around you. With each breath, feel the light warm and brighten you internally.

When you feel calm and centered, move on with your day. Resolve to buy vitamin D and supplement your diet.

Dallas Jennifer Cobb

December

December features a palette of cool colors: white snow, silver icicles, evergreen, and, of course, blue—the bright cerulean sky on a clear, cold winter's day, or the deep navy velvet of the darkening nights, culminating on the longest night of the year, the winter solstice. This hue is reflected in December's birthstones: turquoise, zircon, tanzanite, and lapis. The notion of a stone representing each month has been linked to ayurvedic beliefs that suggest correspondences between the planets and crystals. It wasn't until the eighteenth century that associating stones with a birth month became a popular practice in the Western world.

Even if you weren't born in December, you can still tap into the power of this month's special stones. Zircon increases bone stability, which is good for moving over icy terrain. Use turquoise, a rain-making stone, to summon snow. Turquoise also heals and brings peace. Engage tanzanite's powers for psychic visions for the impending new year. Lapis—the mirror of the winter night sky, and a stone that can be found in the breastplate of the high priest—brings wisdom and awareness.

Natalie Zaman

December 1
Saturday

4th ♏

☽ v/c 9:34 am

☽ → ♎ 9:49 am

Color of the day: Blue
Incense of the day: Sage

Cleaning and Rededicating an Altar

Whether it's a dedicated altar table or a cleared space on a kitchen counter, an altar becomes a focal point of power, and some of this energy remains within the surface after the spell or ritual has concluded. Every so often, it is a good practice to cleanse and rededicate an altar space to clear any magical residue so that it will not confuse the intent of future workings.

A simple means of cleansing is to anoint the altar with saltwater and visualize that this is breaking down any old energy, like dish soap works on a greasy pan. To seal the intention, you can say:

Solid space for magical connection,
renewed, revived, and restored; a clean,
clear focus for fresh direction, my altar
is charged and its power reborn.

Dry off the altar and set any tools back in place.

Michael Furie

December 2
Sunday

4th ♎

Color of the day: Orange
Incense of the day: Marigold

Resolve a Dispute

It's an auspicious day to resolve a dispute, even if the resolution occurs solely within you. Indeed, we must respect the free will of others, and their compliance with or resistance to your efforts need not have any bearing on whether or not you establish inner peace. This does not mean condoning unfair treatment or hurtful actions of any kind. It simply means choosing to let go of the conflict within yourself for your own personal benefit.

So today, hold an unlit stick of frankincense and myrrh incense in your right hand. Feel the discord around the situation and direct it into the incense. Then light it. As the smoke rises, say:

As resin burns to smoke and ash,
I now release the painful past.
Just as day is born from night,
what was heavy now is light.

When it's burned all the way down, scatter the ashes on the wind.

Tess Whitehurst

December 3

Monday

♃ ♎

☽ v/c 1:16 pm

☽ → ♏ 2:55 pm

Color of the day: Ivory
Incense of the day: Narcissus

hanukkah begins

Gossip's Apple

It's tempting to stir the pot, especially when we've been hurt or when someone offends our sensibilities. Make a gossip's apple to warm your heart, still your tongue, and protect you from other wagging tongues! You will need:

- 1 healing apple
- 3 protective star anises
- A jar or two of gossip-stopping cloves
- 4 straight pins (one for each star anise and one to help with the cloves)

Attach each star anise to the apple by driving a pin through the center of the star and into the apple, and speak the first words of the charm:

A star of protection shines on me.

Cover the rest of the apple in cloves, leaving no empty space. Pricking the skin of the apple with the remaining straight pin will help the cloves go in easier. As you insert each clove, say:

A clove for thee, a clove for me.

When you place the last clove, say:

Silence is golden, so mote it be!

Keep the apple where you can see and smell it. Pick it up whenever you feel tempted to stir the pot!

Natalie Zaman

Notes:

December 4

Tuesday

4th ♏

Color of the day: Maroon
Incense of the day: Geranium

Connect to Your Matron Goddess

Whether we've worked with our matron goddess(es) before or not, now, while the solar energies of the year are waning (and the moon is waning as well), is a good time to connect and deepen our bond. We can do devotional rituals, using words of praise and expressions of love.

Whether your matron goddess is an actual matron ("mother"), a maiden, a crone, or some other archetype, you'll want to use a candle in a color you feel would be pleasing to her. Inscribe the candle with words or symbols describing her awesomeness, and meditate on those energies for a while. Think about your special connection with her, and what kinds of energy patterns you would like help with.

When you're ready, light the candle, saying:

I light this candle to represent the
mystery in me that is most like you.
Please, (name of matron goddess),
help me grow more like you every day.

Allow the candle to burn down completely, knowing that as it does so, you are drinking in the light required to understand the depths of her mysteries. Be blessed.

Thuri Calafia

NOTES:

December 5

Wednesday

4th ♏

☽ v/c 4:53 pm

☽ → ♐ 9:49 pm

Color of the day: White
Incense of the day: Lavender

Good Times Ahead

Every year at about this time, it's common to hear people say they can't wait for the year to be over. They then list all of the bad things that happened over the last twelve months. They want a fresh start and believe the new year will bring the good times they crave.

Instead of focusing on the bad things that happened, try focusing on the good things instead. Sometimes we have a very difficult year that makes this task seem impossible, but it can be done. Even if the good things are relatively small compared to the bad events, they should be recognized.

Take a piece of construction or scrapbook paper and make a poster celebrating the good things that happened to you over the past year. Decorate the poster and make it pretty. Place it in a spot where you will see it daily to remind yourself of all the good times you've had and to attract more good ones to you in the coming year.

Kerri Connor

December 6

Thursday

4th ♐

Color of the day: Turquoise
Incense of the day: Balsam

Help! I'm Overbooked!

We're all overbooked. We Pagans love to read. We have so many books on our shelves that our homes are sinking into the ground. What if you're going to get more books as presents over the holidays? It's time to clear your shelves a bit.

Set Athena or other deities of wisdom on your altar and cast a circle around your whole house. Take four grocery bags and contemplate who you'd like to donate some books to—public libraries, charities, covenmates, etc. Write a destination on each bag and ask Athena for guidance as you examine your bookshelves. What books (*The Spiral Dance?*) do you frequently use? Which could you not bear to give away? What books will be useful now to someone else? Select books for each bag. (It's not required that you fill them.) Donate each bag before you change your mind.

Barbara Ardinger

December 7

Friday

4th ♐

New Moon 2:20 am

Color of the day: Purple
Incense of the day: Violet

Open Yourself to the Moon

Today in 1972 was the launch of Apollo 17, the last manned lunar mission. The moon is so captivating that poets write about it, artists paint it, and lygophobics fear it. It plays an important role in astrology and has its place in the tarot's major arcana. The moon plays a part in the earth's "wobble" and pulls at the tides. Some people even respond to the moon's fullness and other phases.

Today is a new moon in Sagittarius, a perfect time for opening yourself to its energy. All you need to do is light a candle and repeat this incantation:

Grandmother Moon, goddess of old,

Throughout the night
your story is told.

By light of the flame and
beat of my heart,

I open my soul, my journey to start.

Pinch out the candle and research all you can about the moon. You'll find her a great companion in your life's journey!

Charlie Rainbow Wolf

 December 8

Saturday

1st ♐

☽ v/c 5:00 am

☽ → ♑ 7:01 am

Color of the day: Black
Incense of the day: Pine

Spell to Increase Freelance Work

It's becoming increasingly common in our "gig economy" to work part-time at multiple jobs, relying on freelance income. It can sometimes be difficult to find more work assignments, especially for people who work with writing, editing, or design, given the recent changes in technology and communication. Our confidence can falter and make us uneasy about finding work. Try this simple spell to help generate more work.

Get a multicolored stack of sticky notes. Write one word on each note that reminds you of how effective and unique your work is. These might be words like "Creative" or "Perfectionist" or "Resourceful." Place these notes around your workspace: above your desk, on your computer monitor, on your bulletin board, on a window, etc. When you see them, say aloud, "I am creative!" and follow up with another related statement, such as "I have great ideas!" This amounts to giving yourself small, frequent pep talks. Change the location of these notes periodically to associate them with different activities.

Peg Aloi

NOTES:

 December 9

Sunday

1st ♑

Color of the day: Gold
Incense of the day: Juniper

Manifesting Your Destiny

We have all probably seen a snowman or created one. By working with the snow, you can manifest your intentions by giving life to a creation. In essence, you are creating the embodiment of your desires. You are welcoming the prospect of your full potential into your life.

Choose the shape of what you are envisioning and shape it with the snow (or shaved ice, if no snow is readily available). Add color with food coloring or scent with essential oils. Once the shape has been created, say:

This creation is what I desire.

As it melts it is what I will acquire.

Place the object you created outside and allow it to melt.

Charlynn Walls

December 10

Monday

1st ♑

☽ v/c 4:27 pm

☽ → ♒ 6:39 pm

Color of the day: Lavender
Incense of the day: Clary sage

hanukkah ends

Witch's Protection Ball

The dark days of winter are a great time to get crafty. Prepare for the upcoming holidays by making some Witch balls. Filled with herbs and decorated with colorful ribbons and charms, they make an enchanting addition to your holiday decor and are a powerful tool in magick.

For this Witch's protection ball, you will need:

- A clear fillable glass ornament
- Spanish moss
- Cinnamon sticks
- Rosemary sprigs
- Dried lavender flowers
- Witchy charms
- Black ribbon

Remove the hanger from the top of the ornament and tuck some Spanish moss, cinnamon sticks, rosemary, and lavender through the opening. Replace the hanger, and add witchy charms around the hanger's base.

Use black ribbon to hang the ornament above a door, on your Yule tree, or over your children's beds. Make Witch balls for any of your magickal needs and keep them out all year round.

Monica Crosson

NOTES:

December 11

Tuesday

1st ♒

Color of the day: Gray
Incense of the day: Ylang-ylang

Five of Wands Spell for holiday Conflict Resolution

The holiday season is here and along with it are the requisite gatherings. Shall we be honest about what we are all thinking? We may not always get along well with all of those people, and the forced interaction with conflicting personalities can be uncomfortable and can often result in conflict. Here is a spell to not only help you keep your own zen but hopefully also keep that of others at your gatherings.

Take an image of the Five of Wands card from the tarot and lay it on your altar on a cloth. The scene on the card is pretty accurate to how some of these gatherings can feel if conflicts ensue. Light a tealight candle and sprinkle some lavender buds over the image while reciting this:

Light of candle, illuminate wisdom divine

Upon me and mine.

Lavender bud, sweet and soothing,

May peace and calm be smoothly moving.

As we gather may it be so,

A happy holiday we shall know!

Blake Octavian Blair

NOTES:

December 12

Wednesday

1st ≈

Color of the day: Brown

Incense of the day: Honeysuckle

Send Me a Message

Wednesdays are ruled by the planet Mercury, the messenger of the gods. If you have something you have been puzzling about, or you aren't sure what choice to make or in what direction to go, then today, turn your indecision, confusion, and lack of clarity over to the gods and goddesses and ask Mercury to bring you a message. State your situation, identify your confusion, and ask the divine powers to send a message regarding which way to turn and what decision to make. Because Mercury oversees daily communication, listen for answers, suggestions, and wisdom in ordinary conversations. Say something like this:

> Universal wisdom, guide me. I'm
> confused and need your help. Should
> I buy a new car now or wait until
> the old car dies and leaves me
> stranded? Send me a message.

Now pay attention to what is said to you and around you today. You may be surprised to receive divine guidance thanks to Mercury.

Dallas Jennifer Cobb

 December 13

Thursday

1st ≈

☽ v/c 5:20 am

☽ → ♓ 7:40 am

Color of the day: Crimson

Incense of the day: Clove

A Prophetic Dream Spell

Perform this spell on a crisp, clear night when the starlight is brilliant. For this spell you'll call upon Asteria, the ancient Greek goddess of shooting stars and prophetic dreams.

On your altar, light one white candle. Decorate your altar with star shapes of your choice. For example, you could use star-shaped holiday ornaments or star-shaped glitter, available at craft stores. Sit in front of the candle and meditate on the prophetic dream you wish to have and the question you want answered. Then call on Asteria:

> Asteria, goddess of prophetic dreams,
> Bring to me the perfect dream
> So that my future can be seen.

Extinguish the candle. To put you in the proper frame of mind to receive a prophetic dream, anoint your forehead with rose water before bed. Or you can mist your pillow with your favorite herbal dream spray. Relax and drift off to sleep. Record any messages you receive in a dream journal.

James Kambos

 December 14

Friday

1st ♓

Color of the day: Rose
Incense of the day: Orchid

Offerings to the Hogboon

My Scottish family lore includes tales of the Hogboon: mound-dwelling fairy folk who lived in Scotland and were particularly active around farmsteads. Like any fae, Hogboons could be mischievous and, if disrespected or displeased, potentially dangerous—or at least rowdy. Conversely, if appeased and honored, they became strong allies, protecting their (and your) home turf against unwelcome visitors and favoring good fortune.

The legends suggest putting out bits of cloth (natural fibers!) and food. A small plate of goodies was shared from every feast meal, and bits of butter, porridge, or cream were left out on non-holidays. Occasionally, a bright red or shiny trinket would be offered.

To work with your own fairy folk, nature spirits, or other local dwellers, leave small offerings, always in the same place and at or near the same times. As you do, speak aloud to the folk and thank them for their role in keeping your grounds safe and secure.

Susan Pesznecker

 December 15

Saturday

1st ♓

☽ v/c 6:49 am

2nd Quarter 6:49 am

☽ → ♈ 7:44 pm

Color of the day: Indigo
Incense of the day: Patchouli

An Inner Look

The longest night of the year is almost here, and introspection is the theme of the season. At night, in a comfortable location, prepare yourself for a deep meditation. You will need a blue candle, some frankincense incense, and some tarot or other oracle cards you like to work with.

Set up your space by lighting the incense and candle, getting comfortable, and setting your intention for internal work. Lay the cards out before you, face down. Let your gaze wash over the cards until you find the one that calls to you. This is the card that you need to meditate on. It is talking to you about your inner self. What story does it tell you? What do you need to appreciate about yourself? What do you need to work on? Between the card you choose and your meditation, you should be able to find the answers.

Kerri Connor

December 16
Sunday

2nd ♈

Color of the day: Yellow
Incense of the day: Almond

The Color of Love

At this time of year, the shops are full of poinsettias. They're a seasonal favorite, but why? Their red and white colors make them very appropriate for seasonal decoration, but the correlation goes much deeper than that.

Poinsettias have long been associated with joy, holiness, and motherhood. That ties them into the Christian Christmas story very well indeed. In fact, there is a legend about a penniless child who had no gifts to bring, so he picked some weeds. As he entered the church, the weeds burst into the bright colors of the poinsettia plants.

With a little care and attention, poinsettias can brighten up your holiday home. Enjoy their color, and bear in mind that when you welcome a poinsettia, you're inviting hope, love, and joy into your life.

Charlie Rainbow Wolf

December 17
Monday

2nd ♈

Color of the day: Silver
Incense of the day: Lily

A Monday Spell of Self-Nurturing

Ah, yes, another Monday. Not everybody likes Mondays because of the common nine-to-five weekday work schedule. Whether or not you follow this schedule, a spell like this can be beneficial for utilizing Monday's nurturing lunar energies rather than giving in to the sometimes chaotic scrambling of the workweek.

The moon, as a planet of classical astrology, is the ruler of Monday. Most ancient cultures associate feminine energies with the moon. Milk is white like the moon and is also the sacred feminine fluid that sustains life. Eggs from all animals are also exclusively part of the feminine domain, and are connected to lunar energies by both shape and color (in many cases).

For this spell, acquire a bit of organic milk and a white egg from a cage-free and humanely raised chicken. (If you are vegan, feel free to substitute however you wish.) Hard-boil the egg and warm up the milk. Sit in a meditative location and, as you consume the egg and milk, repeat the following thirteen times:

> Goddess pure and Goddess
> bright, lend me your healing
> and lend me your light.

Raven Digitalis

NOTES:

December 18
Tuesday

2nd ♈

☽ v/c 2:21 am

☽ → ♉ 4:37 am

Color of the day: Maroon
Incense of the day: Cedar

Spell to Find Your Tribe

Many people believe that our soul mates are twenty to thirty people we incarnate with over and over again from lifetime to lifetime, and that within these groups we've all been each other's parents, friends, lovers, children, clergy members, teachers, and more at one time or another, changing sex and gender with various lifetimes as well. In these troubled times, it can be a great comfort to find those special connections and nurture them.

For this spell, you'll need a cluster crystal with points going out in multiple directions. Cleanse the crystal first with salt water and then, under the waxing moon, hold the crystal up toward the sky. Say:

> My tribe, I'm waiting for you
> here and sending up a light.

> Come be my family once again—
> take the lonely from my nights!

Keep the crystal on your altar and repeat the chant as desired.

Thuri Calafia

December 19

Wednesday

2nd ♉

☽ v/c 7:42 pm

Color of the day: Topaz
Incense of the day: Marjoram

Phoenix Power

The legend of the Phoenix—the fiery bird who combusts into flames, is reduced to ashes, and is reborn—is a powerful spirit to work with. We've all felt, at some time or other in life, as though we've been reduced to ashes and are unsure where we will go from that point. The only thing left to do at that time is to make like the Phoenix and rise! So why not call upon the spirit of the Phoenix for help?

Dress in fiery colors of vibrant reds, oranges, and yellows. Light a candle on your altar and make a prayer to the Phoenix, asking it to assist you and fill you with power if it is willing. Ring a bell, beat a drum, or shake a rattle to welcome it. Continue drumming or rattling, or put on some music. Dance and allow it to fill you with its power!

Blake Octavian Blair

 December 20

Thursday

2nd ♉

☽ → ♊ 9:34 am

Color of the day: Green
Incense of the day: Apricot

Magical Light Display

Many people decorate their houses for Yule (or Christmas) at this time of year, and strings of colorful lights are one of the main forms of decoration. Far from being solely ornamental, these lights can be charged with intention so that the energy they emit is charged to bring peace, joy, and protection through the power of color magic.

Coil a strand of lights so that you can hold it and focus on joyful, positive feelings. Visualize the lights glowing with magical energy, and chant this spell to seal the intention:

Energy spectrum, empowered strand,
a web of power to cover this land;
rainbow of electric light, shine
down blessings through the night;
each color glows with enchanting
charm to increase joy and dispel
harm; this magic so bright for all
to see and as I will, so mote it be.

Put up the lights as soon as possible to unleash the magic.

Michael Furie

December 21
Friday

2nd ♊

☉ → ♑ 5:23 pm

Color of the day: White
Incense of the day: Alder

Yule – Winter Solstice

Yuletide Spell to Plan Winter Work

Yuletide can be festive, but it also is the time when we start to spend more time indoors, especially following the bustle of the holidays. More time indoors in winter means we can make time for projects we don't get to during warmer weather.

For this spell, hand-draw a simple calendar on a piece of paper. Use colored pens and make it eye-catching. Then get some colored sticky notes and write your individual projects on each one (make several for projects that will take more than one day). Keep the project notes on your altar for a night or two, charging them with intention.

Place the project notes on top of the calendar dates on which you plan to do them. If you don't get to it that day, simply move the note to another day. This allows you to be flexible and work according to your own time and energy. Keep the calendar in a visible but accessible place so you can move things as needed.

Peg Aloi

December 22

Saturday

2nd ♊

☽ v/c 9:21 am

☽ → ♋ 11:28 am

Full Moon 12:49 pm

Color of the day: Blue

Incense of the day: Ivy

Full Moon Divination

To scry is to look into water, fire, or some other elemental focus in order to divine the past, present, or future. When the skies are clear and the moon is full, it's a powerful time for moon-scrying.

You'll need a candle and a large silver bowl half-filled with water. You'll work outside, so dress appropriately.

First, place the bowl in a position where, when you're sitting still and looking into the bowl, you can see the full moon's reflection. Once this is arranged, light the candle and set it nearby.

Pause, close your eyes, and envision a question you want answered. When you have this, ask it aloud three times.

Now bend over the scrying bowl, gaze at the moon's reflection, and wait for messages and inspirations—answers to your question. Continue your scrying session until you receive some sort of message.

Immediately afterward, make a dated journal entry about what transpired, and review it every few days. Extinguish the candle.

Susan Pesznecker

NOTES:

December 23
Sunday

3rd ♋

Color of the day: Orange
Incense of the day: Hyacinth

Fairy Lights

One of the joyful—and free!—sights of the season is the displays of lights that go up in the month of December. In stores, in streets, or on homes, they illuminate the night with wishes of goodwill and cheer—and they also attract faeries.

Strings of tiny bulbs glitter like stars, glow light the twilight, and shimmer like all the shiny things fairies like. Tonight when you turn on your light display (or consider making a small display for the fae if you don't put lights up), leave out some small seasonal sweets and invoke the fairies to bless your revels and bring luck in the coming year:

The stars have come to earth,

Come and share our mirth!

Now clap your hands or tap your foot on the ground three times and then continue:

Eat, drink, be merry,

Elf, troll, and fairy!

And bestow upon this place

Love, luck, plenty, and peace.

Blessed be!

Natalie Zaman

December 24
Monday

3rd ♋

☽ v/c 9:50 am

☽ → ♌ 11:59 am

Color of the day: Gray
Incense of the day: Neroli

Christmas Eve

Prophetic Dream Pillow

The new year is just around the corner. What does it have in store for you? Stretch your psychic feelers with a prophetic dream pillow.

Get a drawstring bag or stitch a small pillow from fabric scraps, leaving one side open. Fill with:

2 parts lavender

1 part calendula petals

½ part mugwort

½ part thyme

If you created a pillow, carefully stitch the remaining opening closed.

Enchant your pillow by saying:

Herbs of rest and herbs of dreams,

Help me grasp what is unseen.

Tangled in the web of sleep,

Release for me what I do seek.

Before bed, drink a cup of tea made with equal parts chamomile, lemon balm, and mugwort to help induce psychic dreaming. Tuck the dream pillow near you and enjoy the journey.

Monica Crosson

December 25
Tuesday

3rd ♌

Color of the day: Red
Incense of the day: Ginger

Christmas Day

Release Christmas-Related Negativity

Not everyone loves Christmas. In fact, many of us have quite a bit of emotional baggage attached to it. This spell will help you release old hurtful associations and to see today for the brand-new—and totally neutral—day it truly is. It's great if you can do this at sunrise, but otherwise any time in the morning will do.

Face east and center yourself. Light a stick of cinnamon incense and safely smudge yourself, letting the smoke waft around your body. Hold the incense up to the morning sun. Say:

> *A new day dawns today. It is not like any day that has dawned before. It is fresh, open, and filled with light. I release old cultural and family paradigms, expectations, and emotional hurts. I release the illusion that this day holds any power over me, and I am free. I give thanks for this beautiful day.*

Tess Whitehurst

December 26
Wednesday

3rd ♌

☽ v/c 10:37 am

☽ → ♍ 12:50 pm

Color of the day: Yellow
Incense of the day: Lilac

Kwanzaa begins

Gratitude

The principles of the modern African American festival of Kwanzaa are unity, self-determination, collective work, cooperative economics, purpose, creativity, and faith. As named by Dr. Maulana Karenga, they represent traditional African values.

Because Pagans are not cultural pirates, unless we are part of the African American community, we should not create a Kwanzaa ritual. But we can ask to be invited to a Kwanzaa event or burn red, black, and green candles on our home altar today to support the African American community.

Go online and read about Kwanzaa. Talk to your African American friends about everyday life, especially the good things in life. If your friend is agreeable, take their hands and declare your renewed friendship and support. Say:

> *I'm glad we're friends! I bless your path and my path. It's good that we're together today in peace, honor, and joy.*

Go out to lunch or dinner with your friend.

Barbara Ardinger

NOTES:

 December 27

Thursday

3rd ♍

Color of the day: Purple
Incense of the day: Myrrh

Merging with the Oak

Thursday's energies resonate with the sacred oak tree. Oaks are celebrated as having the spiritual properties of healing, luck, and protection—a winning combination! Today is a good day to make friends with this plant spirit.

Head outdoors and find an oak tree that calls to you. Stand or sit with your back against the tree's trunk. Visualize yourself connecting with the tree. Breathe deeply in and out. See yourself merging with the tree, inviting the tree's spirit within you. See yourself becoming part of the tree. Your legs become roots, your arms become tree limbs, your body becomes covered not in skin but in beautifully textured protective bark. See yourself absorbing the qualities of the oak, healing from the inside out by the tree's spirit, gaining its protection, and perhaps it will share a bit of its luck with you and allow you to take with you the lucky talisman of an acorn.

Blake Octavian Blair

December 28

Friday

3rd ♍

☽ v/c 11:27 am

☽ → ♎ 3:23 pm

Color of the day: Pink
Incense of the day: Rose

Divination with Playing Cards

Today is National Card Playing Day. For a magickal twist on this day, utilize a deck of ordinary playing cards and use them as a divinatory tool. Pull the aces from the deck and lay them out in front of you. Denote one ace to equal "yes," one to equal "no," one to equal "maybe," and one to equal "further clarification needed."

Hold your question in your mind as you begin to turn the cards over, working from left to right. When you get a suit match, that is the answer to your question. This method is great for getting quick answers to questions.

Charlynn Walls

December 29

Saturday

3rd ♎

4th Quarter 4:34 am

Color of the day: Gray
Incense of the day: Sandalwood

We Are One

Psychologist Thomas Lewis talks about limbic resonance, the "symphony of mutual exchange and internal adaptation whereby two mammals become attuned to each other's inner states." Buddhists believe that we are all one consciousness, interconnected and interdependent. As a Pagan, my life is intricately tied to the cycles of the sun, moon, earth, and seasons. Today, practice interconnectedness with all beings. Pause and observe adults, children, and animals. Cultivate compassion. Look respectfully at them, inhale, and draw their energy toward you. Exhale and send acceptance back to them. Inhale and feel their pain, exhaustion, joy, and determination. Exhale and send your serenity, excitement, hope, and resolve. Inhale and exhale and know you are connected. If someone turns and meets your eyes, smile and acknowledge the connection. Think these words as you breathe in and out:

Breathe in: *We are*

Breathe out: *one.*

We are one.

Dallas Jennifer Cobb

December 30

Sunday

4th ♎

☽ v/c 5:53 pm

☽ → ♏ 8:23 pm

Color of the day: Amber
Incense of the day: Eucalyptus

Freeze Negativity in Its Tracks

To freeze negative external forces in their tracks, try this spell. While it won't solve all your problems, this spell aims to help keep these forces from having a harmful influence.

Procure a tight-sealing sandwich bag or freezer bag, along with a teaspoon of vinegar and a pinch of any of these: salt, pepper, chili powder, onion powder, and garlic powder. On a piece of paper, write terms or draw symbols that represent the negative external energy. This could include words such as "sad," "aggression," "hurtful vibes," and anything else you can imagine. You may also draw symbols, mean faces, Xs, and anything else that embodies negative external energies. Whether or not you know the source(s) of these external energies, it's important that your writing capture the feelings you experience as a result.

Place the components in the bag. Crumple the paper and toss it inside, concluding by forcefully spitting into the bag of ingredients. Fill the bag with water. As you seal the bag, say:

Forces of harm from beyond, be gone! By this spell, it shall be done!

Put the bag in a far back corner of your freezer.

In the future, when you feel that the magick is concluded, peel the bag off the ice and place the ice in your toilet to melt.

Raven Digitalis

NOTES:

December 31
Monday

4th ♏

Color of the day: White
Incense of the day: Hyssop

New Year's Eve

New Year's Eve Spell

Tonight we tie a knot on the endless cord of time to signal the end of another year. Use this spell to cleanse yourself and your home so you don't bring negative energy into the new year.

You'll need a bayberry-scented candle, two feet of garden twine, and your cauldron. Light the candle to purify your space. Tie twelve knots in the twine to represent each month. Don't worry if they aren't evenly spaced. Then tie the ends together to symbolize the Wheel of the Year. Now hold the twine and say:

I thank the divine for the good fortune I've had this year,

I face the future without fear.

A year ends, a year begins,

My spirit is renewed as the Wheel turns again.

To release the past, drop the Wheel of the Year that you made with the twine into the cauldron and burn it. Let the candle burn for a while.

James Kambos

NOTES:

Daily Magical Influences

Each day is ruled by a planet that possesses specific magical influences:

Monday (Moon): peace, healing, caring, psychic awareness, purification.

Tuesday (Mars): passion, sex, courage, aggression, protection.

Wednesday (Mercury): conscious mind, study, travel, divination, wisdom.

Thursday (Jupiter): expansion, money, prosperity, generosity.

Friday (Venus): love, friendship, reconciliation, beauty.

Saturday (Saturn): longevity, exorcism, endings, homes, houses.

Sunday (Sun): healing, spirituality, success, strength, protection.

Lunar Phases

The lunar phase is important in determining best times for magic.

The waxing moon (from the new moon to the full moon) is the ideal time for magic to draw things toward you.

The full moon is the time of greatest power.

The waning moon (from the full moon to the new moon) is a time for study, meditation, and little magical work (except magic designed to banish harmful energies).

Astrological Symbols

The Sun	☉	Aries	♈
The Moon	☽	Taurus	♉
Mercury	☿	Gemini	♊
Venus	♀	Cancer	♋
Mars	♂	Leo	♌
Jupiter	♃	Virgo	♍
Saturn	♄	Libra	♎
Uranus	♅	Scorpio	♏
Neptune	♆	Sagittarius	♐
Pluto	♇	Capricorn	♑
		Aquarius	♒
		Pisces	♓

The Moon's Sign

The moon's sign is a traditional consideration for astrologers. The moon continuously moves through each sign in the zodiac, from Aries to Pisces. The moon influences the sign it inhabits, creating different energies that affect our daily lives.

Aries: Good for starting things but lacks staying power. Things occur rapidly but quickly pass. People tend to be argumentative and assertive.

Taurus: Things begun now do last, tend to increase in value, and become hard to alter. Brings out an appreciation for beauty and sensory experience.

Gemini: Things begun now are easily changed by outside influence. Time for shortcuts, communications, games, and fun.

Cancer: Stimulates emotional rapport between people. Pinpoints need, supports growth and nurturance. Tend to domestic concerns.

Leo: Draws emphasis to the self, to central ideas or institutions, away from connections with others and emotional needs. People tend to be melodramatic.

Virgo: Favors accomplishment of details and commands from higher up. Focus on health, hygiene, and daily schedules.

Libra: Favors cooperation, compromise, social activities, beautification of surroundings, balance, and partnership.

Scorpio: Increases awareness of psychic power. Favors activities requiring intensity and focus. People tend to brood and become secretive under this moon sign.

Sagittarius: Encourages flights of imagination and confidence. This moon sign is adventurous, philosophical, and athletic. Favors expansion and growth.

Capricorn: Develops strong structure. Focus on traditions, responsibilities, and obligations. A good time to set boundaries and rules.

Aquarius: Rebellious energy. Time to break habits and make abrupt change. Personal freedom and individuality are the focus.

Pisces: The focus is on dreaming, nostalgia, intuition, and psychic impressions. A good time for spiritual or philanthropic activities.

Glossary of Magical Terms

Altar: A table that holds magical tools as a focus for spell workings.

Athame: A ritual knife used to direct personal power during workings or to symbolically draw diagrams in a spell. It is rarely, if ever, used for actual physical cutting.

Aura: An invisible energy field surrounding a person. The aura can change color depending on the state of the individual.

Balefire: A fire lit for magical purposes, usually outdoors.

Casting a circle: The process of drawing a circle around oneself to seal out unfriendly influences and raise magical power. It is the first step in a spell.

Censer: An incense burner. Traditionally a censer is a metal container, filled with incense, that is swung on the end of a chain.

Censing: The process of burning incense to spiritually cleanse an object.

Centering yourself: To prepare for a magical rite by calming and centering all of your personal energy.

Chakra: One of the seven centers of spiritual energy in the human body, according to the philosophy of yoga.

Charging: To infuse an object with magical power.

Circle of protection: A circle cast to protect oneself from unfriendly influences.

Crystals: Quartz or other stones that store cleansing or protective energies.

Deosil: Clockwise movement, symbolic of life and positive energies.

Deva: A divine being according to Hindu beliefs; a devil or evil spirit according to Zoroastrianism.

Direct/retrograde: Refers to the motion of a planet when seen from the earth. A planet is "direct" when it appears to be moving forward from the point of view of a person on the earth. It is "retrograde" when it appears to be moving backward.

Dowsing: To use a divining rod to search for a thing, usually water or minerals.

Dowsing pendulum: A long cord with a coin or gem at one end. The pattern of its swing is used to answer questions.

Dryad: A tree spirit or forest guardian.

Fey: An archaic term for a magical spirit or a fairylike being.

Gris-gris: A small bag containing charms, herbs, stones, and other items to draw energy, luck, love, or prosperity to the wearer.

Mantra: A sacred chant used in Hindu tradition to embody the divinity invoked; it is said to possess deep magical power.

Needfire: A ceremonial fire kindled at dawn on major Wiccan holidays. It was traditionally used to light all other household fires.

Pentagram: A symbolically protective five-pointed star with one point upward.

Power hand: The dominant hand; the hand used most often.

Scry: To predict the future by gazing at or into an object such as a crystal ball or pool of water.

Second sight: The psychic power or ability to foresee the future.

Sigil: A personal seal or symbol.

Smudge/smudge stick: To spiritually cleanse an object by waving smoke over and around it. A smudge stick is a bundle of several incense sticks.

Wand: A stick or rod used for casting circles and as a focus for magical power.

Widdershins: Counterclockwise movement, symbolic of negative magical purposes, sometimes used to disperse negative energies.

About the Authors

Peg Aloi is a media studies scholar, writer, singer, and professional gardener. She was the Media Coordinator for *The Witches' Voice* from 1997 through 2008. Her blog, *The Witching Hour* (www.patheos.com/blogs /themediawitches), focuses on Paganism and media. She is currently writing a book on the portrayal of witches in film and television.

Barbara Ardinger, PhD (www.barbaraardinger.com, www.facebook.com /barbara.ardinger), is the author of *Secret Lives*, a novel about a circle of crones, mothers, and maidens, plus goddesses, a talking cat, and the Green Man. Her earlier books include *Pagan Every Day*, *Goddess Meditations*, *Finding New Goddesses* (a parody of goddess encyclopedias), and *Quicksilver Moon* (a novel). She is also well known for the rituals she creates. Her day job is freelance editing for people who have good ideas but don't want to embarrass themselves in print. Barbara lives in Southern California with her two rescued Maine coon cats, Heisenberg and Schroedinger.

Blake Octavian Blair is an eclectic Pagan, ordained minister, shamanic practitioner, writer, Usui Reiki Master-Teacher, tarot reader, and musical artist. Blake blends various mystical traditions from both the East and West along with a reverence for the natural world into his own brand of modern Paganism and magick. Blake holds a degree in English and Religion from the University of Florida. He is an avid reader, knitter, crafter, and practicing pescatarian. He loves communing with nature and exploring its beauty. Blake lives in the New England region of the US with his beloved husband. Visit him on the web at www.blakeoctavianblair.com or write to him at blake@blakeoctavianblair.com.

Thuri Calafia is an ordained minister, Wiccan High Priestess, teacher, and author of *Dedicant: A Witch's Circle of Fire* and *Initiate: A Witch's Circle of Water*. She is currently attending Portland State University and working on her third Circles series book, *Adept: A Witch's Circle of Earth*. She lives in the Pacific Northwest with her beloved Labrador, Miss Briana Fae.

Dallas Jennifer Cobb practices gratitude magic, giving thanks for personal happiness, health, and prosperity; meaningful, flexible, and rewarding work; and a deliciously joyful life. She lives in paradise with her daughter, in a waterfront village in rural Ontario, where she regularly swims, runs, and snowshoes. A Reclaiming Witch from way back, Jennifer is part of an eclectic pan-Pagan circle that organizes empowered and beautiful community rituals. Contact her at jennifer.cobb@live.com.

Kerri Connor is the High Priestess of the Gathering Grove. She has written several magic books, including *Spells for Tough Times*.

Monica Crosson is a Master Gardener who lives in the beautiful Pacific Northwest, happily digging in the dirt and tending her raspberries with her husband, three kids, two goats, two dogs, three cats, a dozen chickens, and Rosetta the donkey. She has been a practicing Witch for twenty years and is a member of Blue Moon Coven. Monica writes fiction for young adults and is the author of *Summer Sage*. Her latest book, *The Magickal Family*, will be released by Llewellyn in October 2017.

Raven Digitalis (Missoula, MT) is the author of *Esoteric Empathy, Shadow Magick Compendium, Planetary Spells & Rituals*, and *Goth Craft*. He is a Neopagan Priest and cofounder of an Eastern Hellenistic nonprofit community temple called Opus Aima Obscuræ (OAO). Also trained in Eastern philosophies and Georgian Witchcraft, Raven has been an earth-based practitioner since 1999, a Priest since 2003, a Freemason since 2012, and an empath all his life. He holds a degree in anthropology from the University of Montana and is also a professional Tarot reader, DJ, small-scale farmer, and animal rights advocate. Visit him at www.ravendigitalis .com, www.facebook.com/ravendigitalis, www.opusaimaobscurae.org, or www.facebook.com/opusaimaobscurae.

Michael Furie (Northern California) is the author of *Spellcasting for Beginners, Supermarket Magic*, and *Spellcasting: Beyond the Basics*. His latest book, *Supermarket Sabbats: A Magical Year Using Everyday Ingredients*, will be released by Llewellyn in October 2017. A practicing Witch for more than twenty years, Michael is a priest of the Cailleach. He can be found online at www.michaelfurie.com.

James Kambos is a writer and folk artist who lives in Appalachia. His interest in magic began as a child watching his Greek grandmother perform folk magic. Studying anthropology and sociology in college furthered his interest in magic. He has a degree in history and geography.

Susan Pesznecker is a mother, writer, English teacher, nurse, practicing herbalist, and hearth Pagan living in Oregon. She holds a master's degree in professional writing and loves to read, watch the stars, camp, and garden. Sue has authored *Yule: Rituals, Recipes, & Lore for the Winter Solstice, The Magickal Retreat*, and *Crafting Magick with Pen and Ink* and contributes to the Llewellyn annuals. Visit her on Facebook, www.facebook.com /SusanMoonwriterPesznecker.

Charlie Rainbow Wolf is happiest when she's creating something, especially if it can be made from items that others have cast aside. Pottery, writing, knitting, astrology, and tarot are her deepest interests, but she happily confesses that she's easily distracted because life offers so many wonderful things to explore. A recorded singer-songwriter and published author, she is an advocate of organic gardening and cooking and lives in the Midwest with her husband and special-needs Great Danes. Visit her at www.charlierainbow.com.

Charlynn Walls holds a BA in anthropology, with an emphasis in archaeology. She is an active member of her local community. Charlynn teaches by presenting at various local festivals on a variety of topics. She continues to pursue her writing through articles for *Witches & Pagans* magazine, several of the Llewellyn annuals, and her blog, *Sage Offerings*, at www.sageofferings.net.

Tess Whitehurst is the author of *The Magic of Flowers Oracle* and a number of books about magical living, including *Magical Housekeeping* and *Holistic Energy Magic*. She's also the founder and facilitator of the Good Vibe Tribe, an online magical community and learning hub. Visit her at www.tesswhitehurst.com.

Natalie Zaman is a regular contributor to various Llewellyn annuals. She is the author of the upcoming *Color and Conjure: Rituals and Magic Spells to Color* (Llewellyn, 2017) as well as *Magical Destinations of the Northeast* (October 2016) and writes the recurring feature "Wandering Witch" for *Witches & Pagans* magazine. Her work has also appeared in *FATE*, *Sage Woman*, and *newWitch* magazines. When she's not on the road, she's chasing free-range hens in her self-sufficient and Pagan-friendly back garden. Find Natalie online at http://nataliezaman.blogspot.com.

Spell Notes

Spell Notes

Spell Notes